# EERDMANS'
# ATLAS
## of the
# BIBLE

### WITH A–Z GUIDE TO PLACES

## WM. B. EERDMANS PUBLISHING CO.
255 JEFFERSON AVE. S.E. / GRAND RAPIDS, MICHIGAN 49503

# Contents

## Atlas of the Bible

## A-Z Guide to Places of the Bible

# Note

The *Eerdmans' Atlas of the Bible* combines
two of the ten parts of *Eerdmans' Family
Encyclopedia of the Bible.* Further facts and
geographical information can be found in
other parts of the *Encyclopedia,* especially
*Part 1: Environment of the Bible,* to which there
are a number of cross references.

About the **A-Z Guide to Places of the Bible:**
Entries in the dictionary are followed, where
appropriate, by a cross-reference to the *Atlas.*
The numeral in italic refers to the particular
spread: e.g. 1. *The Land of Israel.* There are
additional grid references to all places shown
on the main *Israel in the Old Testament* and
*Israel in the New Testament* maps.

# Atlas of the Bible

The 'fertile crescent' was a cradle of civilization. It provided the main trade-route to the East and the path for the warring armies which decided the rise and fall of empires.

The plains of Mesopotamia, watered by the Tigris and Euphrates rivers, were the setting for the great empires of Assyria and Babylonia.

The major events of the Bible took place in the land of Israel, at the cross-roads of the ancient world.

Egypt is a constant element in the background to the Bible story, from the time of the patriarchs and the formation of the people of Israel to the time of the prophets – and later as a centre of hellenistic culture in New Testament times.

# 1. The Land of Israel

The land of Israel consists of a 'spine' of hills, with the coastal plain bordering the Mediterranean Sea on one side and the deep Jordan Valley on the other. In the south the land becomes desert. In the north is Galilee, with hills rising to Mt Hermon and the mountains of Lebanon.

Galilee is a region of dry hills and fertile valleys to the west and north of Lake Galilee. Jesus grew up at Nazareth in Galilee. When he began his public work, he spent much of his time teaching and healing here. Many of his closest friends earned their living as fishermen on the lake.

The Carmel hills, running inland from present-day Haifa, bar the way to those travelling along the coast-road. The pass at Megiddo is one of the main breaks in the range, and has always been strongly guarded. Many battles took place on the plain to the north in Old Testament times.

Vines and olives grow on the terraced slopes of the Judean hills. Many famous Bible places – Hebron (Abraham's eventual home), Bethlehem (birthplace of Jesus), Jerusalem – lie in this area.

On the east side of the dry Arabah Valley is the mountainous land of Edom. On their way from Egypt to Canaan the Israelites wanted to pass through Edom, but their request was refused.

The River Jordan, bordered by dense green scrub, winds its way from Lake Galilee to the Dead Sea. It features in many Bible stories: Joshua's crossing into Canaan, the healing of Naaman, and the life of John the Baptist who baptized Jesus in the river.

Farther inland, towards the Jordan Valley and the Dead Sea, the Judean hills become desert – the setting for John the Baptist and the temptations of Jesus.

After their escape from Egypt the Israelites spent forty years in the inhospitable Negev Desert, leading their flocks from place to place in search of food and water.

From Egypt the Israelites travelled to Mt Sinai. This impressive mountain scenery was the background to the covenant-agreement with God, when he gave them his laws and they were declared his people.

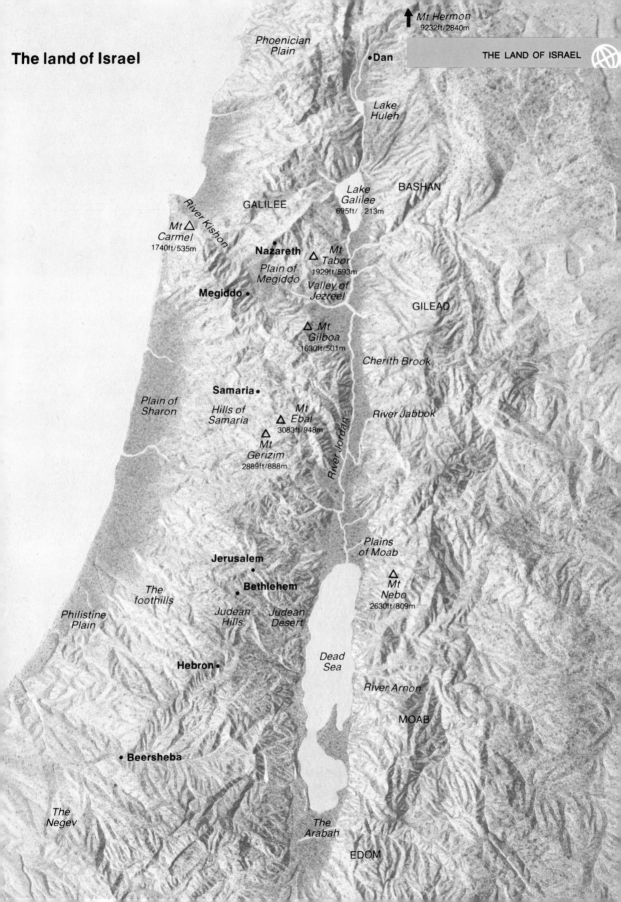

# The land of Israel

Mt Hermon
9232ft/2840m

Phoenician
Plain

•Dan

Lake
Huleh

BASHAN

Lake
Galilee
695ft/ 213m

GALILEE

River Kishon

Mt △
Carmel
1740ft/535m

**Nazareth** •
Plain of
Megiddo

△ Mt
Tabor
1929ft/593m

Valley of
Jezreel

**Megiddo** •

GILEAD

△ Mt
Gilboa
1630ft/501m

Cherith Brook

River Jabbok

Plain of
Sharon

**Samaria** •

Hills of
Samaria

Mt △
Ebal
3083ft/948m

△
Mt
Gerizim
2889ft/888m

River Jordan

Plains
of Moab

**Jerusalem**
•

△
Mt
Nebo
2630ft/809m

The
foothills

• **Bethlehem**

Philistine
Plain

Judean
Hills

Judean
Desert

Dead
Sea

**Hebron** •

River Arnon

MOAB

• **Beersheba**

The
Negev

The
Arabah

EDOM

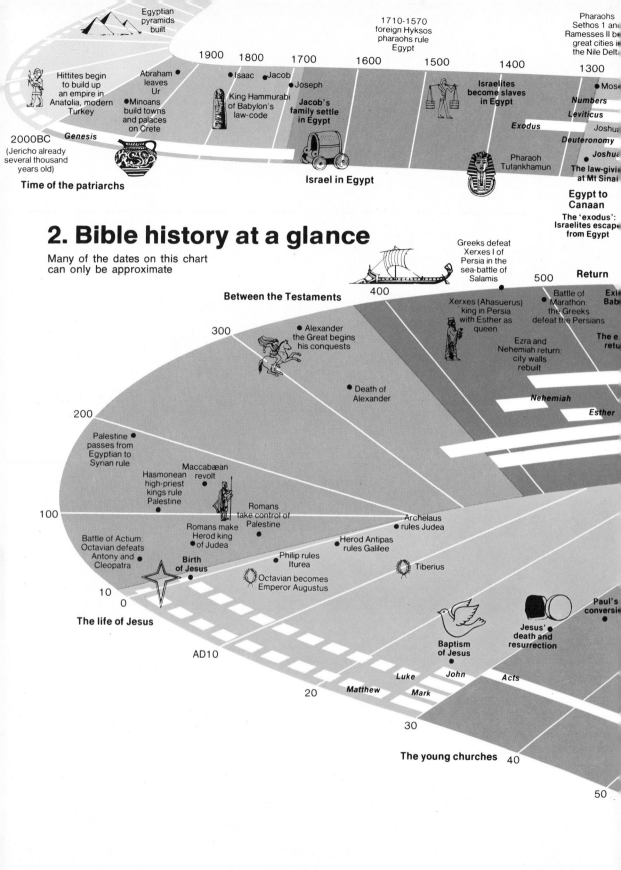

# 2. Bible history at a glance

Many of the dates on this chart can only be approximate

**Egyptian pyramids built**

1710-1570 foreign Hyksos pharaohs rule Egypt

Pharaohs Sethos 1 and Ramesses II b⸱⸱ great cities i⸱ the Nile Delt⸱

1900 1800 1700 1600 1500 1400 1300

Hittites begin to build up an empire in Anatolia, modern Turkey

Abraham leaves Ur

●Isaac ●Jacob

●Joseph

**Israelites become slaves in Egypt**

●Mos⸱

●Minoans build towns and palaces on Crete

King Hammurabi of Babylon's law-code

**Jacob's family settle in Egypt**

*Numbers*

*Leviticus*

*Exodus*

Joshua

*Deuteronomy*

*Joshua*

2000BC (Jericho already several thousand years old)

*Genesis*

Pharaoh Tutankhamun

The law-givi⸱ at Mt Sinai

**Israel in Egypt**

**Time of the patriarchs**

**Egypt to Canaan**

The 'exodus': Israelites escap⸱ from Egypt

Greeks defeat Xerxes I of Persia in the sea-battle of Salamis

500 **Return**

**Between the Testaments**

400

Battle of Marathon: the Greeks defeat the Persians

Exi⸱ Bab⸱

300

●Alexander the Great begins his conquests

Xerxes (Ahasuerus) king in Persia with Esther as queen

Ezra and Nehemiah return; city walls rebuilt

The e⸱ retu⸱

●Death of Alexander

*Nehemiah*

200

*Esther*

Palestine ● passes from Egyptian to Syrian rule

Maccabæan revolt

Hasmonean high-priest kings rule Palestine

Romans take control of Palestine

Archelaus ● rules Judea

100

Romans make Herod king ● of Judea

Herod Antipas rules Galilee

Battle of Actium: Octavian defeats Antony and Cleopatra

●Philip rules Iturea

● Tiberius

**Birth of Jesus**

10

Octavian becomes Emperor Augustus

0

**The life of Jesus**

Jesus' death and resurrection

Paul's conversi⸱

AD10

**Baptism of Jesus**

*Luke*

*John*

*Acts*

20 *Matthew*

*Mark*

30

**The young churches** 40

50

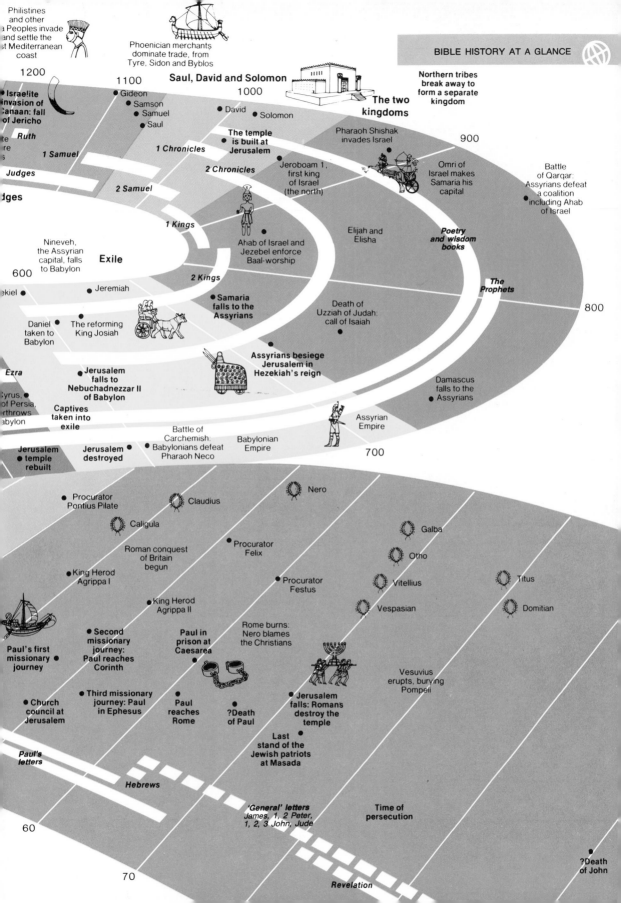

Philistines and other a Peoples invade and settle the st Mediterranean coast

Phoenician merchants dominate trade, from Tyre, Sidon and Byblos

Saul, David and Solomon

Northern tribes break away to form a separate kingdom

1200

1100

1000

900

• Israelite invasion of Canaan: fall of Jericho

• Gideon
• Samson
• Samuel
• Saul

• David
• Solomon

The temple is built at Jerusalem

Pharaoh Shishak invades Israel

Battle of Qarqar: Assyrians defeat a coalition including Ahab of Israel

*Ruth*

*1 Samuel*

*1 Chronicles*

Jeroboam 1, first king of Israel (the north)

Omri of Israel makes Samaria his capital

*Judges*

*2 Chronicles*

*dges*

*2 Samuel*

*1 Kings*

Ahab of Israel and Jezebel enforce Baal-worship

Elijah and Elisha

*Poetry and wisdom books*

Nineveh, the Assyrian capital, falls to Babylon

Exile

*2 Kings*

*The Prophets*

800

600

• Jeremiah

• Samaria falls to the Assyrians

Death of Uzziah of Judah: call of Isaiah

ekiel •

Daniel taken to Babylon

• The reforming King Josiah

Assyrians besiege Jerusalem in Hezekiah's reign

*Ezra*

• Jerusalem falls to Nebuchadnezzar II of Babylon

Damascus falls to the Assyrians

Cyrus, of Persia, rthrows abylon

Captives taken into exile

Battle of Carchemish: Babylonians defeat Pharaoh Neco

Babylonian Empire

Assyrian Empire

Jerusalem temple rebuilt

Jerusalem destroyed

700

• Procurator Pontius Pilate

Claudius

Nero

Caligula

Galba

Roman conquest of Britain begun

Procurator Felix

Otho

• King Herod Agrippa I

Procurator Festus

Vitellius

Titus

Vespasian

Domitian

• King Herod Agrippa II

Rome burns: Nero blames the Christians

Paul's first missionary journey •

• Second missionary journey: Paul reaches Corinth

Paul in prison at Caesarea

Vesuvius erupts, burying Pompeii

• Church council at Jerusalem

• Third missionary journey: Paul in Ephesus

Paul reaches Rome

?Death of Paul

• Jerusalem falls: Romans destroy the temple

*Paul's letters*

Last stand of the Jewish patriots at Masada

*Hebrews*

60

*'General' letters*
*James, 1, 2 Peter,*
*1, 2, 3 John, Jude*

Time of persecution

70

*Revelation*

?Death of John

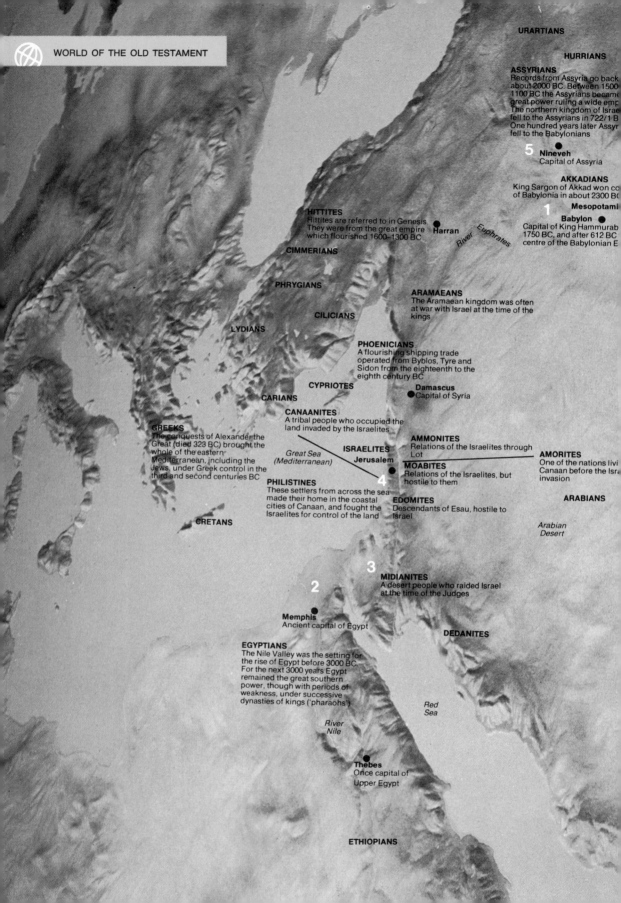

URARTIANS

HURRIANS

**ASSYRIANS**
Records from Assyria go back
about 2000 BC. Between 1500
1100 BC the Assyrians became
great power ruling a wide emp
The northern kingdom of Israe
fell to the Assyrians in 722/1 B
One hundred years later Assyr
fell to the Babylonians

**5** ● Nineveh
Capital of Assyria

**AKKADIANS**
King Sargon of Akkad won co
of Babylonia in about 2300 BC

**1** Mesopotami

Babylon ●
Capital of King Hammurab
1750 BC, and after 612 BC
centre of the Babylonian E

**HITTITES**
Hittites are referred to in Genesis.
They were from the great empire
which flourished 1600–1300 BC
● Harran

*River Euphrates*

CIMMERIANS

PHRYGIANS

**ARAMAEANS**
The Aramaean kingdom was often
at war with Israel at the time of the
kings

CILICIANS

LYDIANS

**PHOENICIANS**
A flourishing shipping trade
operated from Byblos, Tyre and
Sidon from the eighteenth to the
eighth century BC

CYPRIOTES

● Damascus
Capital of Syria

CARIANS

**CANAANITES**
A tribal people who occupied the
land invaded by the Israelites

**GREEKS**
The conquests of Alexander the
Great (died 323 BC) brought the
whole of the eastern
Mediterranean, including the
Jews, under Greek control in the
third and second centuries BC

*Great Sea
(Mediterranean)*

**ISRAELITES**
Jerusalem

**AMMONITES**
Relations of the Israelites through
Lot

**AMORITES**
One of the nations livi
Canaan before the Isr
invasion

**4**

**MOABITES**
Relations of the Israelites, but
hostile to them

**PHILISTINES**
These settlers from across the sea
made their home in the coastal
cities of Canaan, and fought the
Israelites for control of the land

**EDOMITES**
Descendants of Esau, hostile to
Israel

ARABIANS

CRETANS

*Arabian
Desert*

**3**

**MIDIANITES**
A desert people who raided Israel
at the time of the Judges

**2**

● Memphis
Ancient capital of Egypt

DEDANITES

**EGYPTIANS**
The Nile Valley was the setting for
the rise of Egypt before 3000 BC.
For the next 3000 years Egypt
remained the great southern
power, though with periods of
weakness, under successive
dynasties of kings ('pharaohs')

*Red
Sea*

*River
Nile*

● Thebes
Once capital of
Upper Egypt

ETHIOPIANS

**MEDES**
The Median Empire was annexed by Cyrus the Persian in 549 BC

**PERSIANS**
Cyrus the Great established Persian rule over most of the Old Testament world from 539 BC. He allowed the exiled Jews to return home

**ELAMITES**
King Chedorlaomer of Elam took part in a raid on cities in the Jordan Valley at the time of Abraham

● **Susa**
Capital of the Elamite Empire, later an important city under the Medes and Persians

*er Tigris*

**SUMERIANS**
These people were the creators of the Babylonian civilization, leaving us written records from about 3200 BC onwards

**BABYLONIANS**
The history of Babylonia goes back to before 3000 BC. The Babylonians had two periods of great power: about 1850 BC and around 600 BC, the time of King Nebuchadnezzar who destroyed Jerusalem and took its people captive

*Persian
Gulf*

# 3. The World of the Old Testament

**1** The early chapters of **Genesis** are set in Mesopotamia: the garden of Eden, the ziggurat-like Tower of Babel, then the beginning of Abraham's journey to the 'Promised Land', where God would make him a nation and people.

**2** Abraham and the other patriarchs were driven by famine to the richer grain-growing country of Egypt. As the Israelites took on an identity and increased in numbers they became victimized. Eventually they made a bid for freedom under the leadership of Moses, and escaped: the story of **Exodus**.

**3** During the exodus from Egypt to their Promised Land, the Israelites had to spend forty years of hardship in the harsh, mountainous, desert area of the Sinai peninsula. Here God gave them their formative laws, summarized in the books of **Exodus, Leviticus, Numbers** and **Deuteronomy**.

**4** After the conquest of the land of the Canaanites, described in the book of **Joshua**, the Israelites divided the land amongst their ten tribes and settled. They were harassed by surrounding tribes, and the stories of the Israelite champions who defended them are told in **Judges**. The story of their development as a nation, with kings and prophets, is continued in **Samuel, Kings** and **Chronicles** with a background formed by the story of **Ruth** and the books of poetry (**Psalms** and **Song of Songs**) and wisdom literature (**Job, Proverbs, Ecclesiastes**).

**5** The rise of Assyria as one of the threatening 'powers of the north' formed the background to some of the prophets, particularly **Isaiah**. After constant skirmishes and threats of invasion, the people of Israel (the northern kingdom) were taken into exile and Judah (the southern kingdom) narrowly escaped.

**6** The Assyrian Empire gave way to the power of Babylon, to which Judah and Jerusalem eventually fell. This is the background to **Jeremiah**. The prophet **Ezekiel** was one of the exiles, calling the people to remember their God while far away from their own temple. **Daniel** tells the story of a man of God who rose to prominence in the foreign regime. **Ezra** and **Nehemiah** recount stages in the return of the Jews to the land of Israel. The prophets **Haggai** and **Zechariah** also belong to this time.

# 4. The World of Genesis

The Near East before 3000 BC had two quite separate centres of civilization. Each had its own culture, crafts and system of writing. One was in Mesopotamia, the land around the Tigris and Euphrates rivers, part of the 'fertile crescent'. The other was Egypt. The story of mankind begins in Eden, placed somewhere in Mesopotamia. Abraham came from the south Mesopotamian city of Ur. Some of his family settled at Harran in the north while he went on to Canaan.

So the world of Israel's early ancestors was one of rich and powerful kingdoms in the river valleys of Egypt and Mesopotamia. In the lands between were many walled cities and tiny kingdoms. These strongholds protected the settlers who farmed the country around. But there were also nomadic tribespeople who moved from place to place in search of good grazing for their flocks and herds. Abraham and his family were just one group among many on the move in the area.

This was the pattern in Canaan when Abraham arrived to set up camp at Shechem. The coastal

---

Like the modern Bedouin, the desert wanderers, Abraham and his family took their flocks and herds across the desert to find grazing.

plain and the Jordan Valley, where there was good farm land, were already settled. This looked attractive to Abraham's nephew Lot, who moved down from the hills to camp near Sodom. But life there had its dangers. Lot was only one of many who suffered when rebel kings tried to throw off the control of their distant overlords (Genesis 14).

Drought and famine often struck Canaan. So it was natural for the nomads to move down to the fertile land of Egypt. On one occasion (Genesis 12) Abraham was among them. A later famine took the brothers of Abraham's great-grandson, Joseph, to Egypt to buy corn. Soon the whole family of Israel (Jacob's twelve sons) were settled in Goshen, in the eastern Nile Delta. This is where the Book of Genesis ends.

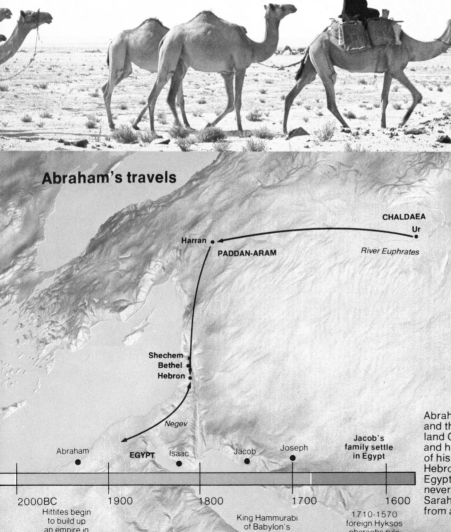

## Abraham's travels

CHALDAEA
Ur

Harran

PADDAN-ARAM          River Euphrates

Shechem
Bethel
Hebron

Negev

Abraham      EGYPT    Isaac          Jacob      Joseph     Jacob's family settle in Egypt

| 2000BC | 1900 | 1800 | 1700 | 1600 |
|---|---|---|---|---|

Hittites begin to build up an empire in Anatolia, modern Turkey

King Hammurabi of Babylon's law-code

1710-1570 foreign Hyksos pharaohs rule Egypt

Abraham came from Ur to Harran and then south-west to Canaan, the land God promised to give to him and his descendants. He spent most of his life in Canaan based near Hebron, apart from a brief visit to Egypt at a time of famine. But he never owned the land. When his wife Sarah died he had to buy ground from a Hittite in order to bury her.

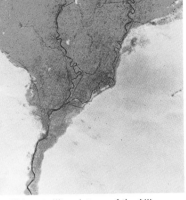

This satellite picture of the Nile Delta, Egypt (photographed on infra-red film) shows as red the crops, trees and plants of the fertile area. Suburban areas, with sparse vegetation, appear as light pink, the desert as light grey, cities dark grey, the waters of the River Nile as blue-black.

Abraham's grandson Jacob, having cheated his brother Esau of his inheritance, left on a hurried visit to relations in Paddan-aram, the district around Harran. For twenty years he worked for his wily uncle Laban. Then he took his two wives and their children, his flocks and herds, and returned home. Jacob was still very much afraid of Esau's anger and at Mahanaim he prayed desperately for God's help. Reassurance came and the reunion was a friendly one. The rest of Jacob's life was spent in Canaan, until in his old age he joined Joseph in Egypt.

Two pictures of Harran today. Here, over 600 miles/960km north-west of Ur, Abraham broke his journey and some of the family settled.

This beautiful inlaid 'Standard of Ur' is just one example of the craftsmanship and skill of the civilized people of Ur even before the time of Abraham. All this was left behind when he set out for Canaan.

## Jacob's journey, and his return home

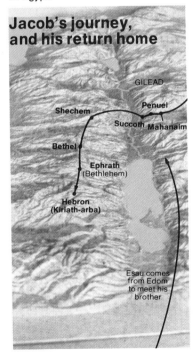

GILEAD

Penuel

Shechem

Succoth  Mahanaim

Bethel

Ephrath
(Bethlehem)

Hebron
(Kiriath-arba)

Esau comes from Edom to meet his brother

## Joseph and his family go to Egypt

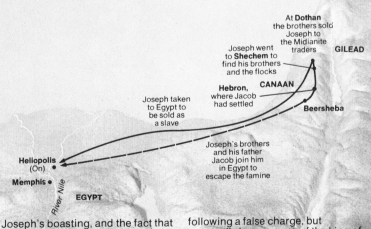

At **Dothan** the brothers sold Joseph to the Midianite traders

Joseph went to **Shechem** to find his brothers and the flocks

GILEAD

**Hebron,** where Jacob had settled

CANAAN

Joseph taken to Egypt to be sold as a slave

Beersheba

Joseph's brothers and his father Jacob join him in Egypt to escape the famine

Heliopolis (On)

Memphis

River Nile

EGYPT

Joseph's boasting, and the fact that he was Jacob's favourite, earned his brothers' hatred. When the opportunity came to get rid of him, they sold him into slavery. Joseph rose to high position in his master's household. He was imprisoned following a false charge, but eventually became one of the king of Egypt's chief ministers. Famine brought the brothers to Egypt, and the whole family was eventually reunited and settled in Egypt near to the court.

# 5. Into the Promised Land

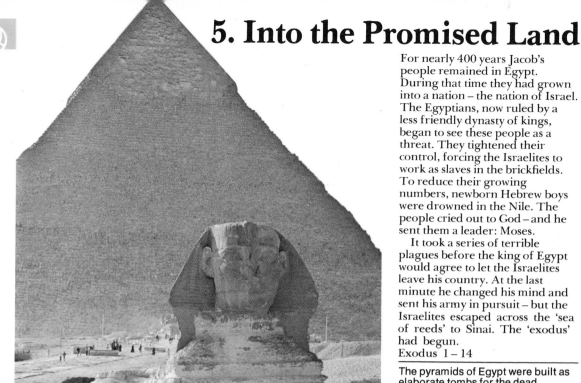

For nearly 400 years Jacob's people remained in Egypt. During that time they had grown into a nation – the nation of Israel. The Egyptians, now ruled by a less friendly dynasty of kings, began to see these people as a threat. They tightened their control, forcing the Israelites to work as slaves in the brickfields. To reduce their growing numbers, newborn Hebrew boys were drowned in the Nile. The people cried out to God – and he sent them a leader: Moses.

It took a series of terrible plagues before the king of Egypt would agree to let the Israelites leave his country. At the last minute he changed his mind and sent his army in pursuit – but the Israelites escaped across the 'sea of reeds' to Sinai. The 'exodus' had begun.
Exodus 1 – 14

The pyramids of Egypt were built as elaborate tombs for the dead pharaohs.

## Out of Egypt into Canaan

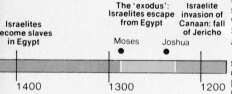

| Israelites become slaves in Egypt | The 'exodus': Israelites escape from Egypt | Israelite invasion of Canaan: fall of Jericho |
| --- | --- | --- |
| | Moses | Joshua |
| 1400 | 1300 | 1200 |

We cannot be certain of the Israelites' route through the Sinai Desert. Numbers 33 lists many places we cannot now locate. But most probably the people travelled south, close to the coast for some way, then inland to the region of Mt Sinai where God gave them his law, and they became his people.

They moved on to Kadesh and sent spies to explore the land of Canaan. The report came back: the land was rich and fertile, but it was a land of walled cities and giant people. When they heard this the Israelites refused point-blank to obey God and go forward. In punishment, they spent forty years in the harsh conditions of the desert.

Then they took the road on the east side of the Arabah Valley, skirting Edom, to fight their first battles with the Amorites and Moabites. They camped on the Plains of Moab across the Jordan from Jericho. Moses died, and Joshua became their new leader.
Exodus 15 – 40; Numbers; Deuteronomy

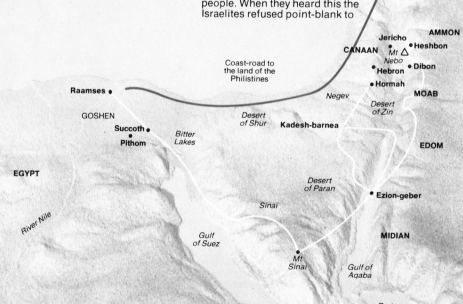

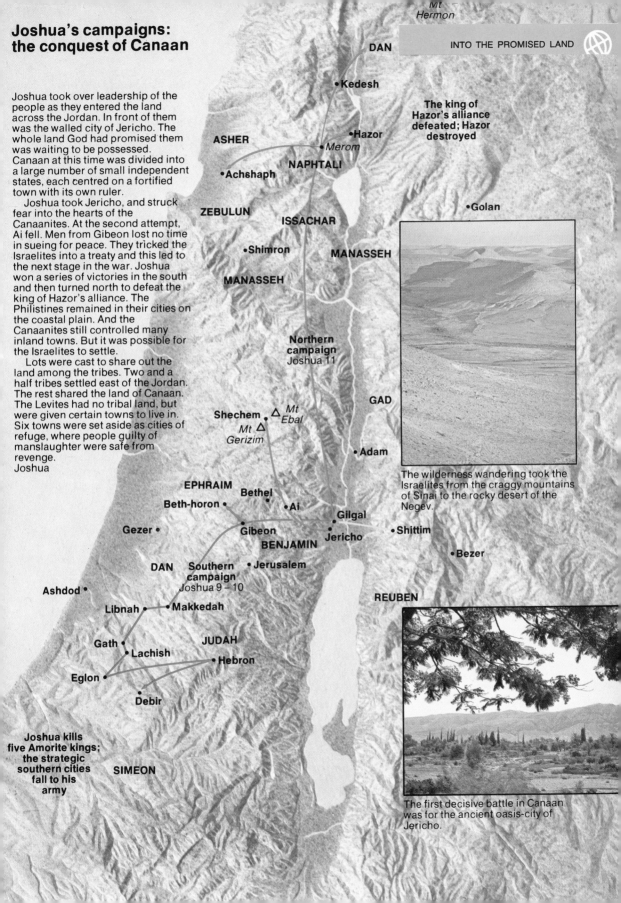

# Joshua's campaigns: the conquest of Canaan

Joshua took over leadership of the people as they entered the land across the Jordan. In front of them was the walled city of Jericho. The whole land God had promised them was waiting to be possessed. Canaan at this time was divided into a large number of small independent states, each centred on a fortified town with its own ruler.

Joshua took Jericho, and struck fear into the hearts of the Canaanites. At the second attempt, Ai fell. Men from Gibeon lost no time in sueing for peace. They tricked the Israelites into a treaty and this led to the next stage in the war. Joshua won a series of victories in the south and then turned north to defeat the king of Hazor's alliance. The Philistines remained in their cities on the coastal plain. And the Canaanites still controlled many inland towns. But it was possible for the Israelites to settle.

Lots were cast to share out the land among the tribes. Two and a half tribes settled east of the Jordan. The rest shared the land of Canaan. The Levites had no tribal land, but were given certain towns to live in. Six towns were set aside as cities of refuge, where people guilty of manslaughter were safe from revenge.
Joshua

**Mt Hermon**

**DAN**

• Kedesh

**ASHER**

• Hazor
• Merom

**NAPHTALI**

• Achshaph

**ZEBULUN**

**ISSACHAR**

• Shimron

**MANASSEH**

**MANASSEH**

Northern campaign
Joshua 11

The king of Hazor's alliance defeated; Hazor destroyed

• Golan

**GAD**

Shechem • △ Mt Ebal
Mt △ Gerizim

• Adam

The wilderness wandering took the Israelites from the craggy mountains of Sinai to the rocky desert of the Negev.

**EPHRAIM**
Bethel •
Beth-horon • • Ai
Gilgal •
Gezer • Gibeon • Jericho •
**BENJAMIN**
• Shittim

**DAN** Southern campaign
Joshua 9 – 10
• Jerusalem

• Bezer

**REUBEN**

Ashdod •
Libnah • • Makkedah
Gath • **JUDAH**
• Lachish • Hebron
Eglon •
• Debir

**Joshua kills five Amorite kings; the strategic southern cities fall to his army**

**SIMEON**

The first decisive battle in Canaan was for the ancient oasis-city of Jericho.

# 6. The Judges

The tribes settled into the areas allotted to them. They were scattered now, and surrounded by hostile neighbours. Joshua was dead. It began to seem impossible to gain full control of the land. Gradually the Israelites lost sight of the fact that God was fighting for them. They began to compromise with the nations around, and with their gods, for the sake of peace. Their enemies took advantage of their evident weakness. The Book of Judges relates the sad story.

The surrounding nations returned to the attack: the king of Mesopotamia from the north; Moabites and Ammonites from across the Jordan; Midianites from the east. The Canaanites at Hazor grew strong enough to make a second attack on the settlers. And from the coastlands the Philistines pushed the Israelites further and further into the hills.

As at so many times in their history, the Israelites cried to God for help in their need. Each 'Judge' won at least a temporary respite. The most famous of these freedom-fighters are Deborah and Barak, Gideon, Jephthah and Samson.

## Barak and Gideon
Judges 4 – 7

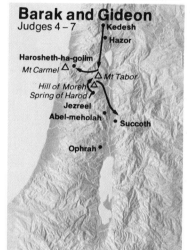

- Kedesh
- Hazor
- Harosheth-ha-goiim
- Mt Carmel
- Mt Tabor
- Hill of Moreh
- Spring of Harod
- Jezreel
- Abel-meholah
- Succoth
- Ophrah

## Samson's daring raids
Judges 13 – 16

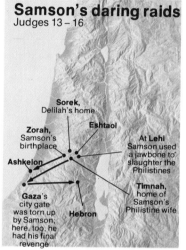

- Sorek, Delilah's home
- Eshtaol
- Zorah, Samson's birthplace
- At Lehi Samson used a jawbone to slaughter the Philistines
- Ashkelon
- Timnah, home of Samson's Philistine wife
- Gaza's city gate was torn up by Samson; here, too, he had his final revenge
- Hebron

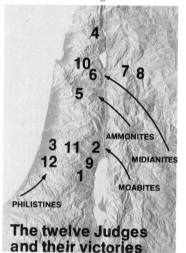

- 4
- 10
- 6
- 7  8
- 5
- 3  11  2
- 12  9
- 1
- AMMONITES
- MIDIANITES
- MOABITES
- PHILISTINES

## The twelve Judges and their victories

1. **Othniel** of Judah defeated Cushan-rishathaim
2. **Ehud** of Benjamin killed King Eglon of Moab
3. **Shamgar** defeated the Philistines
4. **Deborah** (from Ephraim) and Barak (from Naphtali) defeated Jabin and Sisera
5. **Gideon** of Manasseh defeated the Midianites and Amalekites
6. **Tola** of Issachar
7. **Jair** of Gilead
8. **Jephthah** of Gilead defeated the Ammonites
9. **Ibzan** of Bethlehem
10. **Elon** of Zebulun
11. **Abdon** of Ephraim
12. **Samson** of Dan fought the Philistines

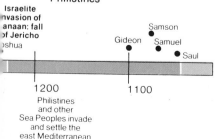

Israelite invasion of Canaan: fall of Jericho — Joshua

Gideon — Samson — Samuel — Saul

1200    1100

Philistines and other Sea Peoples invade and settle the east Mediterranean coast

Not long after they settled in Canaan the Israelites began to worship the local gods, especially Baal the weather-god.

Remains of the city of Ashkelon, the Philistine stronghold which features in Samson's exploits.

**Israel in the Old Testament**

A B C 1

Abel-beth-maacah
Tyre
Dan

Ramah
Kedesh
Maacah

1

Hazor
Merom

Chinnereth
BASHAN

GALILEE
Sea of Chinnereth
Ashtaroth

2

△ Mt Carmel
River Kishon
Plain of Jezreel
Gath-hepher
△ Mt Tabor
Edrei

Shunem
Endor
Jezreel
Lo-debar
Ramoth-gilead

Dor
Megiddo
GILEAD

3

Taanach
Mt Gilboa △
Beth-shan

Sharon
Ibleam
Dothan
Abel-meholah

Cherith Brook

Samaria
Tirzah
Jabesh-gilead
Succoth
Mahanaim
Penuel

Plain of Sharon
△ Mt Ebal
Shechem
△ Mt Gerizim

River Jordan

4

Aphek
ISRAEL
Shiloh
Adam
AMMON

Joppa
Timnath-serah
Jazer

Upper/Lower Beth-horon
Bethel
Ai
Michmash
Rabbah

Gibeon
Mizpah
Gilgal
Shittim

Gezer
Sorek
Gibeah
Geba
Heshbon

Ekron
Aijalon
Anathoth
Jericho

Timnah
Kiriath-jearim
Jerusalem
△ Mt Nebo

5

Eshtaol
Bethlehem

Ashdod
Libnah
Zorah
Makkedah
Wilderness of Judah
Salt Sea (Sea of the Arabah)

PHILISTIA
Azekah
Tekoa
Ataroth

Ashkelon
Valley of Elah
Adullam
Keilah
Kiriathaim
Dibon

Beth-zur
Aroer

Mareshah
Hebron
Engedi

Gaza
Lachish
Eglon

MOAB

Gerar
Ziklag
Maon
JUDAH

Beersheba
Arad
Ar

Hormah

Kir-hareseth

Ziph

Negev Desert

0 10 20 30 40 Km
0 5 10 15 20 25 M

# 7. Israel's First Kings: Saul, David and Solomon

## David's wars
2 Samuel 8; 10; 1 Chronicles 18 – 20

The last and greatest of the Judges was Samuel – prophet and king-maker. When Samuel grew old, the people asked for a king to rule them, like the other nations. Samuel warned them that a king would mean conscription to the army, forced labour and oppression. But the Israelites insisted. And at last Samuel did as they asked.

The first king was a tall, handsome Benjaminite called Saul. To begin with all went well. But power went to Saul's head and he began to disregard God's clear instructions. Because of Saul's disobedience, his son Jonathan did not inherit the throne. Instead, during Saul's lifetime, God sent Samuel to anoint David as Israel's next king.

While still just a shepherd-boy, David killed the Philistine champion, Goliath. His popularity made Saul jealous, and for a number of years David was forced to live as an outlaw, in danger of his life. Then Saul and Jonathan were killed in battle against the Philistines. David became king.

David united the kingdom, captured Jerusalem, the Jebusite stronghold, and made it his capital. He was a soldier-king. During his lifetime he expanded the kingdom and drove off old enemies. His legacy to his son Solomon was peace and security.

David wanted to build a temple for God in Jerusalem, but he had to be content with getting materials together. It was Solomon who built the temple, and many other fine buildings. A strong, secure kingdom made it possible for Solomon to prosper through trade alliances. His wisdom was legendary. At Solomon's court there was leisure for culture and beauty. His reign was Israel's golden age.

But there was another side to the picture. The introduction of heavy taxes, forced labour and foreign gods sowed the seeds that were to divide the kingdom after his death.
1 Samuel 8 – 1 Kings 11

**PHILISTINES**

David defeats the Philistines and ends their control over the land

Timeline:
Gideon — Samson — Samuel — Saul — David — Solomon — Jeroboam 1 first king of Israel (the north)

1100 — 1000 — 900

The temple is built at Jerusalem

Northern tribes break away to form a separate kingdom

Mt Gilboa, where Saul and his son Jonathan died.

## Saul's campaigns

No sooner had he become king than Saul was faced with a challenge from the Ammonites who moved in to besiege Jabesh. He gathered an army and launched a three-pronged attack which drove them off. Following this, and all through his life, there was war with the Philistines. Although he succeeded to some extent in keeping them at bay, in the end they defeated and killed him in battle on Mt Gilboa.

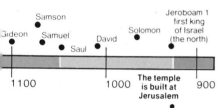

**Aphek**
Philistines gather

**Endor**
Saul consults a medium

**Beth-shan**
Saul's body nailed to the city wall; rescued by men from Jabesh

Battle of Gilboa: Saul and Jonathan killed

**Shunem**

Mt Gilboa
Israelite camp

Valley of Jezreel

**Bezek**
Saul sets out from Gibeah; gathers an army at Bezek, and routs the Ammonites

**Jabesh-gilead**

**AMMON**
King Nahash of Ammon sets out to attack Jabesh

Philistines camp at Michmash: raids to Ophrah, Beth-horon, Zeboiim

### Saul's last campaign
1 Samuel 28; 31

Jonathan defends the pass at Michmash

## Campaign against the Ammonites
1 Samuel 11

**Rabbah**

**Michmash**

**Aljalon**

**Mizpah**
Saul proclaimed king

**Gibeah**

**Gilgal**
Saul proclaimed king again

**Geba**
Jonathan kills Philistine commander

Saul wins further victories against the people of Edom, Ammon, Moab and Amalek

### War against the Philistines
1 Samuel 13 – 14

Philistine troops move north to camp near Shunem

Tyre
of Hamath makes peace with David
Dan
David defeats King Hadadezer of Zobah, in Syria
The Syrians of Damascus become David's subjects

Kadesh

David defeats the Syrian army at Helam

Rabbah

Jazer
AMMONITES

David's army, under Joab, defeats the Ammonites and Syrians at Rabbah. He puts the people to forced labour

Gezer

Jerusalem

ath

Aroer

MOABITES

The Moabites become David's subjects

Hebron

Beersheba

EDOMITES

David defeats the Edomites in the Valley of Salt

David was made king at Hebron, but for two years he was king only of Judah. At the pool of Gibeon he met the Israelites supporting Saul's family, and defeated them. Gradually he won control of the whole country. Then he began to wage war on enemies round about, extending his land in all directions.

## King Solomon's administration
1 Kings 4

'Solomon's kingdom included all the nations from the River Euphrates to Philistia and the Egyptian border. They paid him taxes and were subject to him all his life.' Peace and security freed the king to attend to other affairs, among them government and administration.

At the local level he appointed twelve district governors, each responsible for supplying the court with food for one month each year. They reported to the governor of the whole land. In addition there were court secretaries, a records officer, adviser, palace steward and minister in charge of forced labour.

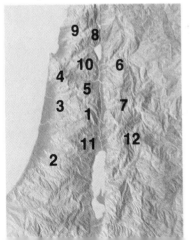

9  8
10  6
4
5
3  7
1
11  12
2

## The wealth of King Solomon
1 Kings 5; 10

'King Solomon was richer and wiser than any other king.' He extended his capital Jerusalem, built the city wall and added many fine buildings besides the temple. He built up a large force of chariots and horses. Hazor, Gezer and Megiddo were rebuilt. So too were 'Lower Beth-horon, Baalath, Tamar in the wilderness of Judah, the cities where his supplies were kept, the cities for his horses and chariots, and everything else he wanted to build in Jerusalem, in Lebanon, and elsewhere in his kingdom'.

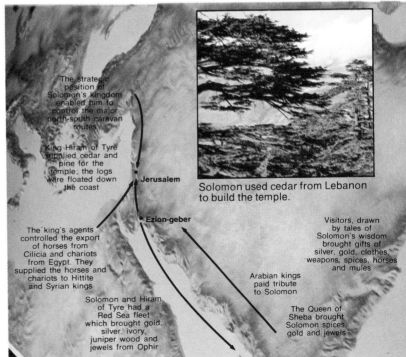

The strategic position of Solomon's kingdom enabled him to control the major north-south caravan routes

King Hiram of Tyre supplied cedar and pine for the temple; the logs were floated down the coast

Jerusalem

Solomon used cedar from Lebanon to build the temple.

Ezion-geber

The king's agents controlled the export of horses from Cilicia and chariots from Egypt. They supplied the horses and chariots to Hittite and Syrian kings

Solomon and Hiram of Tyre had a Red Sea fleet which brought gold, silver, ivory, juniper wood and jewels from Ophir

Visitors, drawn by tales of Solomon's wisdom brought gifts of silver, gold, clothes, weapons, spices, horses and mules

Arabian kings paid tribute to Solomon

The Queen of Sheba brought Solomon spices, gold and jewels

# 8. The Two Kingdoms

Under King Solomon Israel became a rich and powerful kingdom, but the people were oppressed and burdened with heavy taxes and forced labour. When Solomon's son Rehoboam came to the throne they appealed to him to lighten their burdens. He refused. The ten northern tribes rebelled. They set up a new kingdom, the kingdom of Israel, with Jeroboam I ruling as king from his capital at Shechem. In the south, Rehoboam ruled the kingdom of Judah (the tribes of Judah and Benjamin) from Jerusalem.

Jeroboam also had to set up a new centre of worship for the northern kingdom, now cut off from Jerusalem. He chose Dan, in the north, and Bethel, an important centre when Samuel was alive. But pagan practices quickly became part of the worship. The historians who wrote **Kings** and **Chronicles** classified the kings as 'good' or 'bad' depending on whether they reformed religion or let the pagan practices continue.

Uzziah and Hezekiah were two of the reforming kings of Judah. King Ahab of Israel had one of the worst records. He and his foreign wife Jezebel opposed Elijah and persecuted those who worshipped God. The remains of his 'ivory house' at Samaria can be seen today (see Part 2: *Archaeology and the Bible*). Assyrian annals record that he brought 10,000 men and 2,000 chariots to the Battle of Qarqar, where he joined forces with the Egyptians to resist the Assyrian King Shalmaneser (853 BC).

Mt Carmel, where Elijah staged his contest with the prophets of Baal, juts into the sea behind the present-day port of Haifa (below).

Afterwards Elijah ran before the king's chariot to the palace at Jezreel.

Jeroboam 1 first king of Israel (the north)

Ahab of Israel and Jezebel enforce Baal-worship

Death of Uzziah of Judah call of Isaiah

900

800

Northern tribes break away to form a separate kingdom

Omri of Israel makes Samaria his capital

Damascus falls to the Assyrians

## Elijah

Zarephath

Mt Carmel

Jezreel

Tishbe
Cherith Brook

Samaria

Beersheba

To Mt Horeb (Sinai)

## Elisha

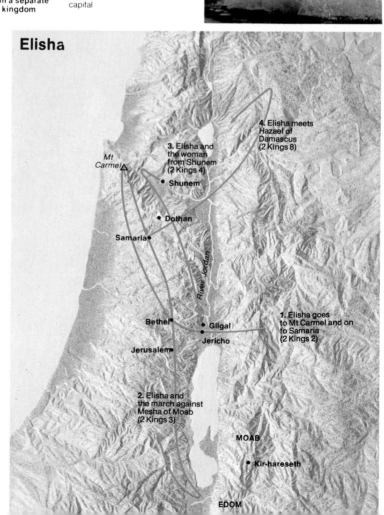

Mt Carmel

Shunem

Dothan

Samaria

Bethel

Gilgal

Jericho

Jerusalem

River Jordan

4. Elisha meets Hazael of Damascus (2 Kings 8)

3. Elisha and the woman from Shunem (2 Kings 4)

1. Elisha goes to Mt Carmel and on to Samaria (2 Kings 2)

2. Elisha and the march against Mesha of Moab (2 Kings 3)

MOAB

Kir-hareseth

EDOM

# The kingdoms of Israel and Judah

**SYRIA**

**Tyre**
Queen Jezebel's
home

**Abel-beth-maacah**

**Dan**
Israel's
cult centre in
the north

**Kedesh**

Syrian attack

Combined armies
of Egypt, Israel and
Syria march to
Qarqar to fight the
Assyrians

**Hazor**

Intermittent
attacks from Syria
900-800 BC (1 Kings 15; 2 Kings 6 – 7)

**Acco**

**Chinnereth**

*River Kishon*

*Mt Carmel*
Scene of
Elijah's contest
with the
prophets of Baal

**Ramoth-gilead**

**Dor**

**Shunem**
Elisha stayed
here

**Megiddo**

**Jezreel**
Jezebel died
here

△ *Mt Gilboa*

Ahab (Israel) and
Jehoshaphat (Judah)
set out to re-capture
Ramoth-gilead from
the Syrians but are
defeated
(1 Kings 22)

**Taanach**

**Beth-shan**

**ISRAEL**

**Ibleam**

**Dothan**

**Samaria**
Capital of
Israel

**Tirzah**

**Jabesh-gilead**

**Penuel**

**Succoth**

**Mahanaim**

**Shechem**
Israel's first
capital

*River Jordan*

**Aphek**

**Bethel**
Israel's
southern cult
centre

**Shiloh**

**AMMON**

**Joppa**

**Mizpah**

**Ramah**

**Gibeon**

**Geba**

**Gilgal**

**Jericho**

**Gezer**

**Ekron**

**Aijalon**

**Gibeah**

**Jerusalem**
Capital
of Judah

**Ashdod**

**Bethlehem**

**Beth-shemesh**
Here Jehoash of
Israel defeated
Amaziah of Judah

**Tekoa**

**PHILISTIA**

Ashkelon

**Gath**

**Mareshah**

**Lachish**
Here Amaziah
of Judah died

**Hebron**

*River Arnon*

Gaza

**Ziph**

**En-gedi**

**JUDAH**

**MOAB**

**Gerar**

**Beersheba**

Zerah the
Ethiopian attacks
Judah; King Asa
defeats him at
Mareshah
(2 Chronicles 14)

Joram (Israel)
and Jehoshaphat (Judah)
march against Mesha
of Moab
(2 Kings 3)

Shishak of
Egypt attacks
Jerusalem
(1 Kings 14:25)

**Kir-hareseth**

**EDOM**

# 9. The Rise of the Northern Powers

Israel and Judah, in their strategic position between Egypt and the Mesopotamian powers, were very vulnerable to aggression. David and Solomon were successful partly because none of the larger nations were powerful enough to attack during their reigns. But after the division of the kingdom the nations immediately around – Syria, Ammon, Moab – gave the subsequent kings of Israel and Judah increasing trouble. However, it was the growth of the major powers farther north-east that proved decisive.

The Assyrian Empire had an earlier period of power under Tiglath-pileser I. But the ruthless aggression for which Assyria was so much feared reached its peak in the period between 880 and 612 BC. The empire was based on three great cities: Asshur, Calah and Nineveh.

From the mid-ninth century BC, the time of Ahab in Israel, the kings of Assyria repeatedly attacked Israel and Judah. Soon King Jehu of Israel was paying tribute to Shalmaneser III of Assyria. A hundred years later Ahaz of Judah asked Tiglath-pileser III of Assyria to help him fight Syria and Israel (Isaiah 7; 2 Kings 16). He did so and defeated them both, but Judah had to become a subject kingdom of the Assyrians in return for their help.

When Israel refused to pay their yearly tribute, the next king of Assyria took Samaria, exiled the people and destroyed the northern kingdom (722/1 BC; 2 Kings 17). Soon after this, Egypt was defeated by the Assyrians. In 701 BC the powerful King Sennacherib besieged Jerusalem, but because of King Hezekiah's trust in God the city was saved (2 Kings 19).

The Assyrians had to fight many battles to defend their empire. In the next century several provinces regained their freedom. The empire lasted until Asshur fell to the Medes in 614 and Nineveh was destroyed by the Medes and Babylonians in 612.

## Phase 1

● In 853 BC Shalmaneser's army was confronted at Qarqar by twelve kings who had come together to oppose him: one was Ahab of Israel.
● In 841 BC Shalmaneser again marched on the area, laying siege to Damascus. Jehu of Israel paid him tribute. Shalmaneser then had to secure his northern borders against attack, and Damascus seized the opportunity of attacking Israel and Judah.

## Phase 2

● A century later Assyria regained power. King Tiglath-pileser III invaded the area in 743 BC and each year after that. King Azariah of Judah paid him tribute. The Assyrians increasingly adopted the policy of taking subject people into exile.
● Tiglath-pileser campaigned as far as 'the brook of Egypt' in 734 BC. Then in 733 he attacked Israel, destroying Megiddo and Hazor and turning the coastal plain, Galilee and the area beyond the Jordan into Assyrian provinces.
● In 732 BC Samaria was spared only because their rebellious King Pekah was assassinated (2 Kings 15:27-31).
● Shalmaneser V captured Hoshea, king of Israel in 724 BC, and laid siege to Samaria (2 Kings 17:4). He took it in 722 BC.
● In 722/1 BC Sargon II despoiled the city of Samaria, carried off the cream of the population into exile, and so destroyed the northern kingdom of Israel (2 Kings 17:5).

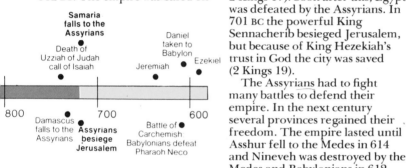

Samaria falls to the Assyrians

Death of Uzziah of Judah call of Isaiah

Daniel taken to Babylon

Jeremiah

Ezekiel

800    700    600

Damascus falls to the Assyrians

Assyrians besiege Jerusalem

Battle of Carchemish Babylonians defeat Pharaoh Neco

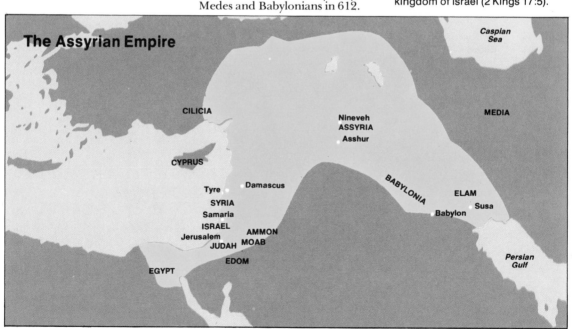

**The Assyrian Empire**

Caspian Sea

CILICIA

Nineveh
ASSYRIA
Asshur

MEDIA

CYPRUS

Tyre   Damascus

SYRIA

Samaria

ISRAEL

Jerusalem

JUDAH   MOAB

AMMON

EDOM

EGYPT

BABYLONIA

ELAM

Susa

Babylon

Persian Gulf

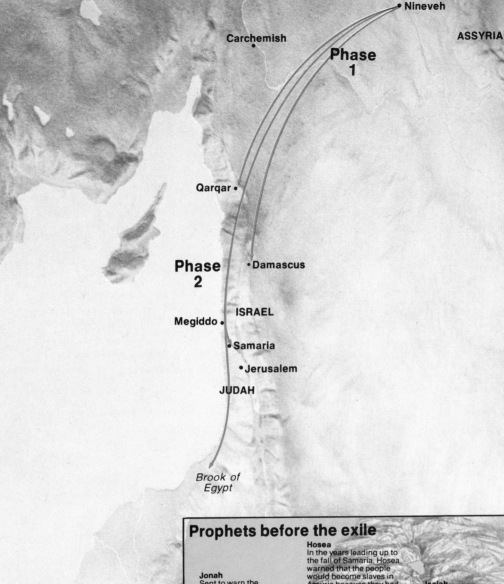

Nineveh

Carchemish

ASSYRIA

**Phase 1**

Qarqar

**Phase 2**

Damascus

ISRAEL

Megiddo

Samaria

Jerusalem

JUDAH

*Brook of Egypt*

EGYPT

## Prophets before the exile

**Jonah**
Sent to warn the inhabitants of Nineveh of God's judgement. As a result, the people changed their ways and God spared the city

**Hosea**
In the years leading up to the fall of Samaria, Hosea warned that the people would become slaves in Assyria because they had forgotten God. They had even turned to Assyria and Egypt for help

**Isaiah**
Lived in Jerusalem at the time when Judah was threatened by the Assyrians. Looked ahead not only to the conquest of Jerusalem by the Babylonians but to a future age of peace

• Samaria

**Micah**
Warned of the Assyrian and Babylonian invasions; predicted the fall of both Samaria and Jerusalem

• Jerusalem

**Zephaniah**
Lived during Josiah's reign. Condemned the worship of Canaanite and Assyrian gods. Predicted disaster for the pagan nations around. Foretold the destruction and restoration of Jerusalem

**Nahum**
Predicted the destruction of Nineveh as a judgement on the Assyrians for their cruel treatment of other nations

**Amos**
Born in Judah but prophesied in Israel during the reign of Jeroboam II. Condemned Israel's neighbouring countries for their cruelty. Warned that the Israelites would be taken captive by the Assyrians

# 10. Invasion and Exile

If Assyria in the Bible meant oppression, Babylon meant power. Nabopolassar, governor of the area around the Persian Gulf, freed Babylon from the Assyrians and in 626 BC was made king. He continued to gain victories over the Assyrians and in 612 BC the Babylonians and Medes captured the Assyrian capital of Nineveh. They were not content with taking over Assyria itself but set out to conquer the whole Assyrian Empire.

The Assyrians retreated to Harran but were soon driven out. The Egyptians, realizing that their own country might be in danger, marched north to support them. King Josiah of Judah intercepted the Egyptian army at Megiddo. In the resulting battle he was killed and Judah became subject to Egypt (2 Kings 23:29). Four years later, in 605 BC, the Babylonian army led by Nebuchadnezzar defeated the Egyptians at Carchemish (Jeremiah 46:1-2). The Babylonian Empire was spreading. Jehoiakim of Judah was one of the many kings who now had to pay tribute to Nebuchadnezzar.

After a fierce battle with the Babylonians in 601 BC the Egyptians encouraged Judah to rebel. Nebuchadnezzar sent troops to crush the rebellion and in 597 BC, shortly after Jehoiachin had become king, Judah submitted. The king and many of the country's leaders were taken into exile in Babylon. The policy of the invaders was not just to plunder and destroy, but also to weaken the subject nations and prevent further rebellions by deporting their leading citizens (2 Kings 24:10-17).

Despite this, ten years later Zedekiah, a puppet king placed on the throne of Judah by Nebuchadnezzar, appealed to the Egyptians for help. The Babylonians invaded Judah and laid siege to Jerusalem. The siege lasted eighteen months. Finally, a breach was made in the walls. In 586 BC the city was taken. King Zedekiah was captured and blinded. Valuable objects including the temple treasure were taken to Babylon. Jerusalem and its temple was destroyed and the citizens deported. Only the very poor were left to cultivate the land (2 Kings 25:1-21).

● In 609 BC King Josiah of Judah was killed at Megiddo. He was opposing the Egyptian army which was marching in support of Assyria against the increasing threat of the Babylonians and Medes.

● Nebuchadnezzar of Babylon, having defeated the Egyptians at Carchemish, made Judah a subject state in 605 BC, and occupied the coastal plain.

● Jehoiakim of Judah tried to enlist the help of Egypt against Babylon in 601 BC following the battle between Pharaoh Neco and King Nebuchadnezzar.

● Jerusalem was forced to surrender to Nebuchadnezzar in 598 BC, and leading citizens were exiled to Babylon.

● Ten years later Nebuchadnezzar again marched on Jerusalem following a rebellion. In 586 BC the city was taken and destroyed, and the citizens were taken into exile.

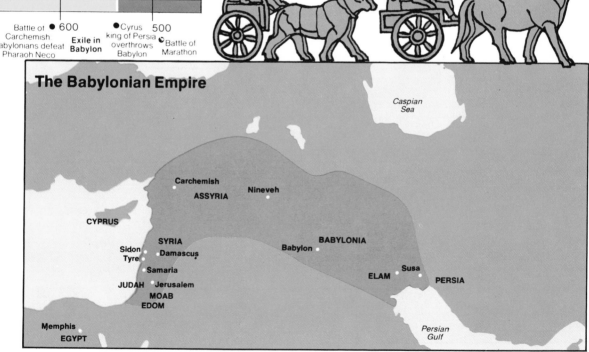

Daniel taken to Babylon ● Ezekiel ●
Jeremiah ●     Jerusalem falls

Battle of ● 600     ● Cyrus 500
Carchemish                king of Persia ◐ Battle of
Babylonians defeat  Exile in  overthrows  Marathon
Pharaoh Neco       Babylon   Babylon

## The Babylonian Empire

Caspian Sea

Carchemish
ASSYRIA     Nineveh

CYPRUS

SYRIA          BABYLONIA
Sidon  Damascus    Babylon
Tyre
Samaria            Susa
JUDAH  Jerusalem   ELAM  PERSIA
MOAB
EDOM

Memphis                Persian Gulf
EGYPT

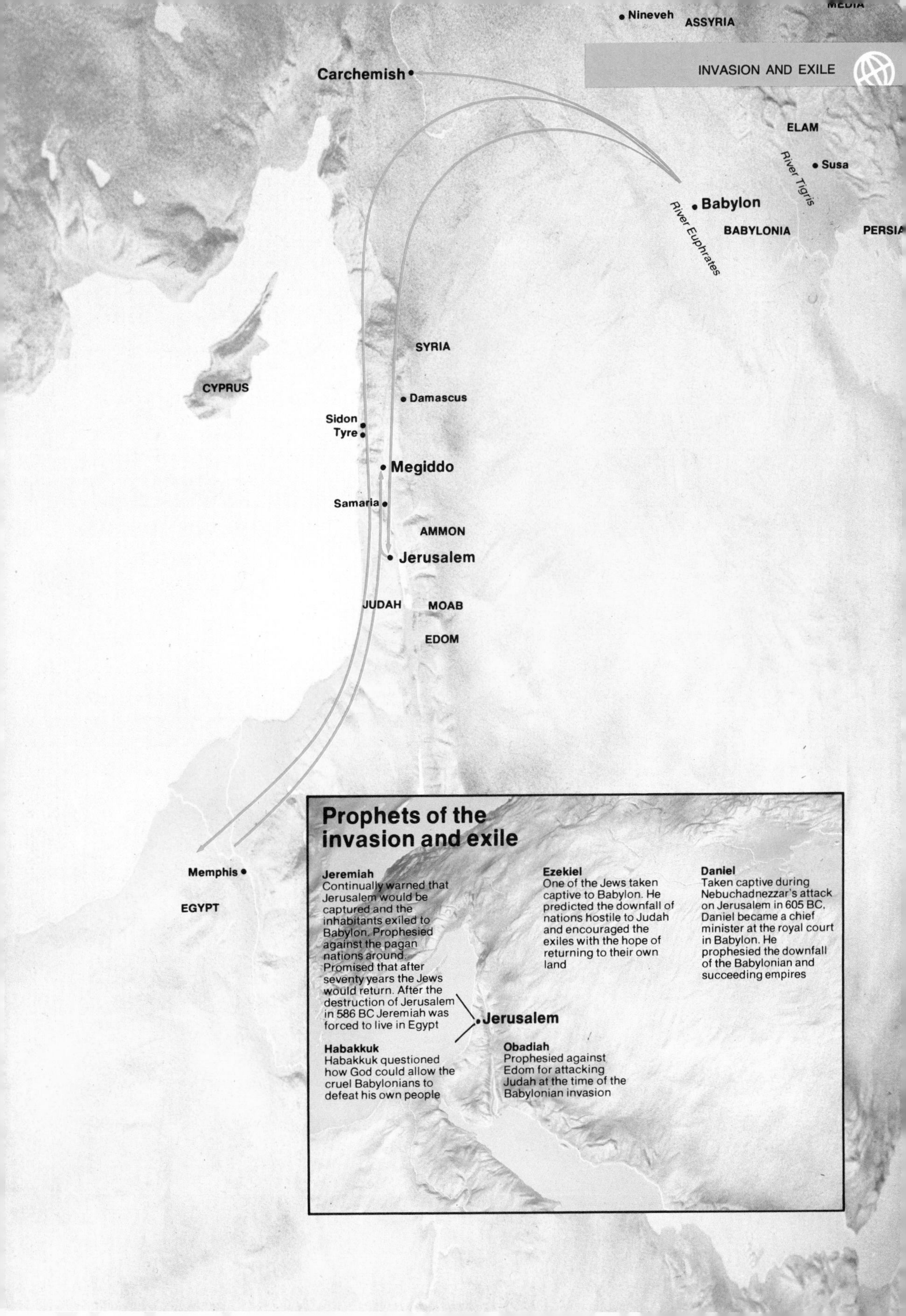

MEDIA

Nineveh • ASSYRIA

Carchemish •

ELAM

• Susa

River Tigris

• Babylon

BABYLONIA

PERSIA

River Euphrates

SYRIA

CYPRUS

• Damascus

Sidon •
Tyre •

• Megiddo

Samaria •

AMMON

• Jerusalem

JUDAH    MOAB

EDOM

Memphis •

EGYPT

## Prophets of the invasion and exile

**Jeremiah**
Continually warned that Jerusalem would be captured and the inhabitants exiled to Babylon. Prophesied against the pagan nations around. Promised that after seventy years the Jews would return. After the destruction of Jerusalem in 586 BC Jeremiah was forced to live in Egypt

**Ezekiel**
One of the Jews taken captive to Babylon. He predicted the downfall of nations hostile to Judah and encouraged the exiles with the hope of returning to their own land

**Daniel**
Taken captive during Nebuchadnezzar's attack on Jerusalem in 605 BC, Daniel became a chief minister at the royal court in Babylon. He prophesied the downfall of the Babylonian and succeeding empires

• Jerusalem

**Habakkuk**
Habakkuk questioned how God could allow the cruel Babylonians to defeat his own people

**Obadiah**
Prophesied against Edom for attacking Judah at the time of the Babylonian invasion

# 11. Return to Jerusalem

In the first half of the sixth century BC Babylon appeared all-powerful. But the prophets spoke of a God to whom kings were as puppets, and who could use even pagan powers to fulfil his purposes.

Cyrus the Persian united the two kingdoms of Media and Persia to the east of Babylon. He conquered lands as far east as India. Then he attacked Babylon. The city fell in 539 BC and he took over the whole empire.

The Persian kings extended their borders even further than the earlier empires. They took Egypt and all of what is now Turkey. When Babylon fell, Cyrus began to reorganize the empire. He divided it into provinces, each with its own ruler, called a 'satrap'. These were mainly Persians, but under them were local rulers who retained some power. The different peoples were encouraged to keep their own customs and religions.

As part of this policy, Cyrus sent the Jews back to Jerusalem to restore the city and rebuild the temple, as told in the books of **Ezra** and **Nehemiah**. Jews also settled in many other parts of the empire. In Susa, one of the Persian capitals, a later king, Xerxes I, even made a Jewess his queen, as told in the book of **Esther**. The 'dispersion', as Jews living in other lands came to be called, was significant later, in New Testament times. Because they were away from the temple, these Jews developed the local synagogue as a centre of teaching and worship. And this laid the basis for the later rapid spread of the Christian churches, which were formed on this model.

King Darius I (522-486), builder of the great new capital, Persepolis, and conqueror of western India, also pushed the empire westwards. In 513 he took Macedonia in northern Greece. In 490 the Persians were defeated by the Greeks at Marathon, and the stage was set for some of the greatest stories of Greek classical antiquity. Xerxes I (486-465) invaded Greece, even occupying

**1** The Persians adopted a policy of allowing subject peoples to remain in their own lands. In 538 BC the first exiles returned to Judah. Soon after this, under Zerubbabel's leadership, they began to rebuild Jerusalem.

**2** Nehemiah led another group of exiles back to Jerusalem where they helped rebuild the city walls. Ezra returned to Jerusalem to re-emphasize the Law of God, renew worship and to set the Jewish community in order.

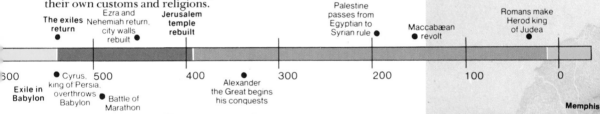

Mediterranean Sea

Memphis

Timeline:
- The exiles return
- Ezra and Nehemiah return, city walls rebuilt
- Jerusalem temple rebuilt
- Palestine passes from Egyptian to Syrian rule
- Maccabæan revolt
- Romans make Herod king of Judea

- 600 | Exile in Babylon
- Cyrus, king of Persia, overthrows Babylon · 500 · Battle of Marathon
- 400 · Alexander the Great begins his conquests
- 300
- 200
- 100
- 0

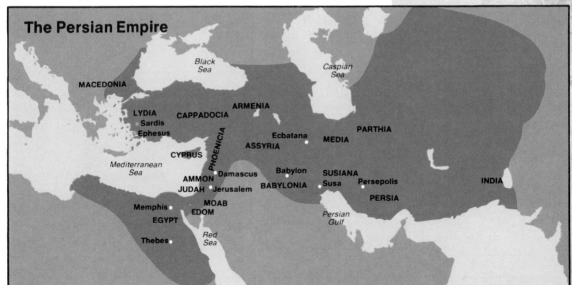

## The Persian Empire

MACEDONIA
Black Sea
Caspian Sea
LYDIA
Sardis
Ephesus
CAPPADOCIA
ARMENIA
PARTHIA
PHOENICIA
CYPRUS
Ecbatana
MEDIA
ASSYRIA
Mediterranean Sea
AMMON
Damascus
Babylon
SUSIANA
JUDAH
Jerusalem
BABYLONIA
Susa
Persepolis
INDIA
PERSIA
MOAB
EDOM
Memphis
Persian Gulf
EGYPT
Thebes
Red Sea

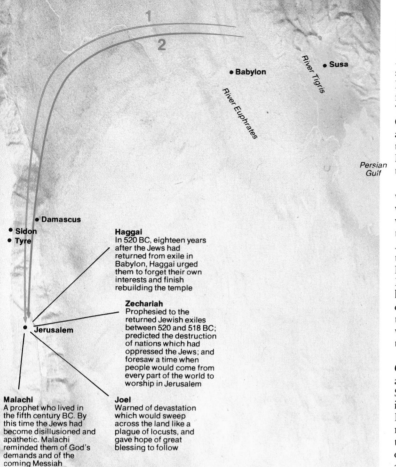

**Haggai**
In 520 BC, eighteen years after the Jews had returned from exile in Babylon, Haggai urged them to forget their own interests and finish rebuilding the temple

**Zechariah**
Prophesied to the returned Jewish exiles between 520 and 518 BC; predicted the destruction of nations which had oppressed the Jews; and foresaw a time when people would come from every part of the world to worship in Jerusalem

**Malachi**
A prophet who lived in the fifth century BC. By this time the Jews had become disillusioned and apathetic. Malachi reminded them of God's demands and of the coming Messiah

**Joel**
Warned of devastation which would sweep across the land like a plague of locusts, and gave hope of great blessing to follow

Athens, but was defeated in the sea battle of Salamis. Artaxerxes, Darius II, and the kings that followed, took up the struggles. The fortunes of Persia and Greece, Media and Egypt ebbed and flowed until finally, in 333 BC, the Greek soldier Alexander of Macedon crossed the Hellespont to begin his meteoric career.

Alexander was only twenty-two when he set out on a campaign which swept across the ancient world. He 'liberated' Egypt from the Persians (founding the port of Alexandria), then marched east, to the heart of the Persian Empire. He pressed on as far as India, conquering all who stood in his way and founding Greek city-states wherever he went. His title 'Alexander the Great' was well earned. He died, when only thirty-three, in 323 BC.

Following his death, the great Greek Empire was divided up among his four generals. The Seleucid rulers, based on Antioch in Syria, controlled Palestine. The Ptolemies, based on Alexandria, ruled Egypt. Culturally, however, the Greek or 'hellenistic' world continued as a unity, with Greek as a common language and with a common pattern of civilization. This background played a vital part in events which were to follow: the events of the New Testament.

**The Greek Empire**

# 12. Jerusalem

At the time the Israelites entered their Promised Land, Jerusalem was held by a local tribe, the Jebusites. It remained in their possession until King David sent his men up through the water tunnel to take the stronghold. 'After capturing the fortress, David lived in it and named it "David's City". He built the city round it, starting at the place where land was filled in on the east side of the hill.'

Jerusalem became David's capital, and he built himself a palace there. His son Solomon built the temple. He also built himself a new palace with a great hall (the Hall of the Forest of Lebanon, presumably so named because of its rows of cedar pillars), a 'hall of columns' and a throne or judgement room as well as private quarters. He filled in land on the east side of the city and built the city wall.

King Hezekiah, under threat of an Assyrian siege, engineered a tunnel to bring water from the Gihon Spring inside the city wall. This prevented the enemy from cutting off the water supply. (See Part 2: *Archaeology and the Bible*.)

Despite its excellent position and defences Jerusalem fell to the army of Nebuchadnezzar of Babylon in 586 BC. Solomon's temple was burnt. So too were the palace and the houses of the wealthy. Nebuchadnezzar's soldiers tore down the city walls. All the temple treasures were taken away. 'How lonely lies Jerusalem, once so full of people,' wrote the author of Lamentations. 'The Lord rejected his altar and deserted his holy Temple; he allowed the enemy to tear down

its walls. The gates lie buried in rubble, their bars smashed to pieces.'

It remained in ruins for fifty years, until the first exiles returned. Then slowly, over a period of about a hundred years, the city, temple and walls were rebuilt. This was the city of the second temple, shown in these photographs of a model at the Holyland Hotel, Jerusalem. A sketch-map shows the probable extent of the city in the time of Nehemiah.

Nebuchadnezzar had attacked the city from the north, its weakest defensive position. Between Nehemiah's time and AD 70, when Titus took Jerusalem for

the Romans, three walls were built to guard the northern part of the city. After the death of Alexander the Great, the Jews became subjects of the Syrian Seleucid kings, who had a garrison in Jerusalem.

The Greeks gave way to the Romans, and the Romans placed Herod the Great on the throne. Herod rebuilt the temple on a very grand scale and during his reign the city also gained many new public buildings, a hippodrome, theatre, amphitheatre and baths. The model shows the scale of the temple in relation to the size of Jerusalem in New Testament times.

## Jerusalem at the time of the kings

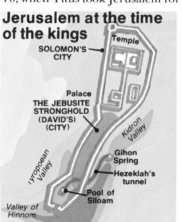

SOLOMON'S CITY
Temple
Palace
THE JEBUSITE STRONGHOLD (DAVID'S) (CITY)
Kidron Valley
Tyropoean Valley
Gihon Spring
Hezekiah's tunnel
Pool of Siloam
Valley of Hinnom

## Jerusalem in Nehemiah's time

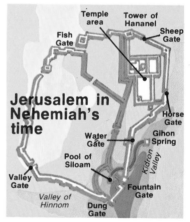

Temple area
Tower of Hananel
Fish Gate
Sheep Gate
Horse Gate
Water Gate
Gihon Spring
Pool of Siloam
Valley Gate
Valley of Hinnom
Dung Gate
Fountain Gate
Kidron Valley

A model of Fort Antonia, the Roman garrison close to the temple in Jerusalem.

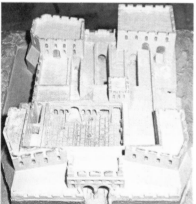

## Jerusalem in New Testament times

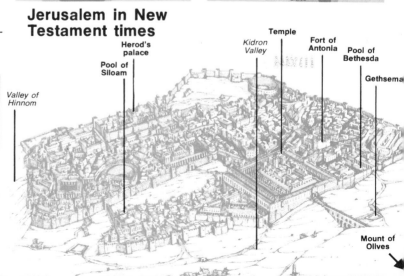

Valley of Hinnom
Herod's palace
Pool of Siloam
Kidron Valley
Temple
Fort of Antonia
Pool of Bethesda
Gethsema
Mount of Olives

Jerusalem stands on a flat-topped hill about 2700ft/830m above sea level. In David's day and later it was almost surrounded by deep ravines. But over the centuries, as the city spread westwards, the Tyropoean ('Cheesemakers') Valley was gradually filled in. Today, although the western Hinnom Valley and eastern Kidron Valley show clearly from the air, the Tyropoean Valley can hardly be seen. This picture, taken from the south, shows the present wall of the old city, and temple area.

## Jesus in Jerusalem

Jesus first went to Jerusalem as a boy, going to the Passover Festival with his parents. He quickly found his way to the Jewish teachers in the temple. As an adult he attended many of the religious festivals in the city and often taught there himself. The sight of money-changers and people selling animals for sacrifice in the temple courtyard called forth the angry words: 'Stop making my Father's house a market-place.'

In Jerusalem he invited all who were 'thirsty', to 'come to me and drink'. In Jerusalem he declared himself to be 'the light of the world'. In Jerusalem, at the Pool of Bethesda (Bethzatha), he healed a man who had been ill for thirty-eight years. At Jerusalem he gave sight to a man born blind, telling him to wash his face in the Pool of Siloam.

When he came to Jerusalem Jesus often stayed over the hill at Bethany, with his friends Mary and Martha and their brother Lazarus. On the way there, just across the Kidron Valley from the temple, was the Garden of Gethsemane, where he could find quiet to pray.

In Jerusalem the world-shaking events of the last week of his life took place. Here Jesus was crucified, at a place called 'The Skull' outside the city wall. Here he rose from the grave, victorious over sin and death. From the Mount of Olives he returned to his Father in heaven, his work on earth completed.

Remains of the Pool of Bethesda (Bethzatha), deep below the present level of Jerusalem.

The Garden of Gethsemane.

The Mount of Olives.

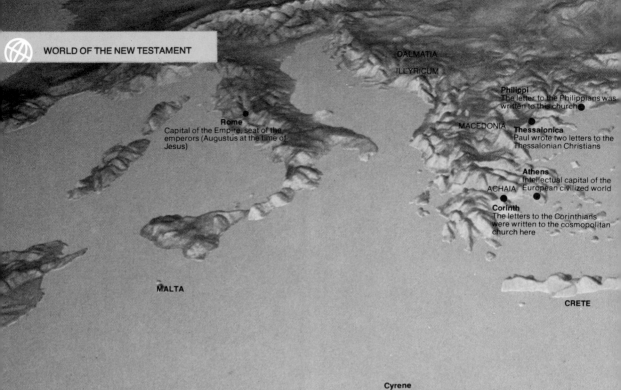

DALMATIA

ILLYRICUM

**Philippi**
The letter to the Philippians was
written to this church

**Rome**
Capital of the Empire, seat of the
emperors (Augustus at the time of
Jesus)

MACEDONIA

**Thessalonica**
Paul wrote two letters to the
Thessalonian Christians

**Athens**
Intellectual capital of the
European civilized world

ACHAIA

**Corinth**
The letters to the Corinthians
were written to the cosmopolitan
church here

**MALTA**

**CRETE**

**Cyrene**

# 13. The World of the New Testament

The spread of Greek culture
(hellenism) and the fact that many
Jews were dispersed in other
lands had set the scene for the
New Testament. The final key
factor was Roman rule, which
unified the ancient world
politically, just as hellenism
unified it culturally.

So the time was ripe for the
coming of Jesus. The Jews from
many countries who were in
Jerusalem to hear the Christian
good news could go there because
of the Roman peace. The
Christian missionaries could
travel to the main centres quickly
because of the Roman roads. Paul
was both a Jewish scholar and a
Roman citizen.

The Roman conquest of the
Greek Empire was completed in

the first century BC. What had
been the national art, literature
and philosophy of Greece now
became the more cosmopolitan
'hellenism', the language and
culture that were expressed in
such a surprising number of great
cities. The ruins of many of these
can still be admired today:
Palmyra, out in the Syrian desert;
or Ephesus, where Paul spent two
years preaching and teaching.

The religions of classical
antiquity had become bankrupt:
so the time was ripe for the
Christian gospel too. The old gods
of Greece and Rome had merged
with the mystery religions, the
traditional pagan religions of the
rural areas (the worship of earth
and fertility gods) and a general
awareness of a world of spirits.

After the philosophy of the
Greeks and the materialism of the
Romans, people were searching
for more 'spiritual' answers: but
all too often they simply lapsed
into superstition.

Archaeologists exploring
hellenistic cities such as Sardis, in
present-day Turkey, have been
surprised to discover large Jewish
synagogues. In an age of
degenerate religion, many
non-Jews were attracted to the
Jewish faith and became
'God-fearers'. And Jews living
abroad had laid a foundation of
belief in God and knowledge of
the Law of God in many places.
Jesus came, as the author of the
letter to the Hebrews expressed it,
'when the time was ripe'.

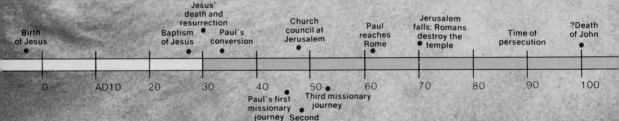

Birth
of Jesus

Jesus'
death and
resurrection

Baptism
of Jesus

Paul's
conversion

Church
council at
Jerusalem

Paul
reaches
Rome

Jerusalem
falls: Romans
destroy the
temple

Time of
persecution

?Death
of John

0    AD10    20    30    40    50    60    70    80    90    100

Paul's first
missionary
journey

Third missionary
journey

Second
missionary
journey

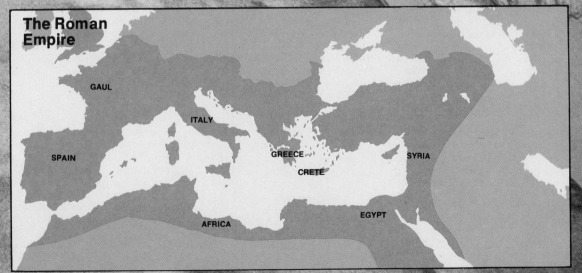

**roas**
te of ancient Troy

BITHYNIA
and PONTUS

GALATIA
Paul wrote Galatians to the
Christians here

PISIDIA

CAPPADOCIA

ASIA

**rgamum**

CILICIA

PAMPHYLIA

**Tarsus**
Birthplace of Paul

**Antioch**
Capital of the Seleucid Greek
kings and a major city; one of the
leading churches was here

**Ephesus**
A major centre
of hellenistic
culture: Paul
wrote the letter to
the Ephesians to
the Christians
here

LYCIA

**Miletus**

SYRIA

**Palmyra**

CYPRUS

**Damascus**

**Caesarea**
Built as a port
by the Romans

**Jerusalem**

PALESTINE
The events of the Gospels took
place in Galilee and Judea

**Alexandria**
A main centre of hellenistic
culture and residence of the
Ptolemies; the Old Testament was
translated into Greek here

NABATAEA

**Petra**

EGYPT

## The Roman Empire

GAUL

ITALY

SPAIN

GREECE

SYRIA

CRETE

AFRICA

EGYPT

# 14. Israel in the New Testament

By New Testament times the Jewish people had lived under foreign occupation for some 500 years since returning to their own land. Under Greek rule they had paid tribute to Ptolemy of Egypt and adopted Greek as the language of the empire. In 198 BC

Galilee was the scene of much of the teaching of Jesus. Several of his closest followers were fishermen from Lake Galilee. For a time he was based on the lakeside town of Capernaum.

the Seleucid Greek ruler of Syria, Antiochus the Great, defeated the Ptolemies and took Palestine. But he in turn was defeated by the Romans at Magnesia in 190 BC.

The Romans taxed the Seleucid Empire harshly, and they in turn took any opportunity to loot cities and temples. Antiochus Epiphanes used the opposition of loyal Jews, the 'Hasidim' or 'pious ones', as an excuse to plunder the Jerusalem temple. Later he built a pagan Greek centre in the heart of the city and in the temple an altar to Zeus on which pigs (forbidden under Jewish food laws) were sacrificed.

This final affront resulted in the Maccabean Revolt. The Jews succeeded in freeing themselves for a time and were able to cleanse and rededicate the temple in 165 BC. The high priest Aristobolus, a later member of the Hasmonean family which had led the revolt, declared himself king in 104 BC. But before long,

rivalries among the Jews gave the Romans the chance to intervene. The last high-priest king was executed in 37 BC.

Judea became subject to Rome under the governor of the province of Syria. But the Jews kept the freedom to practice their religion and had their own ruler: from 37 to 4 BC an Idumean Jew named Herod. Despite his ambitious building projects – including a new temple in Jerusalem – the Jews hated Herod the Great, and he is chiefly remembered for his tyranny and cruelty.

This was the background to the birth of Jesus. Luke records the fact that Jesus was born in the

The Galilee countryside.

time of the first Roman Emperor, Augustus. He was succeeded by Tiberius in AD 14. Herod's act in putting the children of Bethlehem to death was wholly in character with what we know of him otherwise. When he died, the kingdom was divided among three of his sons. One ruled so badly that the Romans removed him and appointed a 'prefect' for Judea. Pontius Pilate, who passed the death sentence on Jesus, was prefect AD 26-36.

The Jewish council, the Sanhedrin, tried to keep the peace

## Herod's kingdom

ITURAEA
GALILEE TRACHONITIS

DECAPOLIS

SAMARIA

PEREA

JUDEA

IDUMAEA

NABATAEA

with the Romans to protect its own position. Others, such as the hated tax collectors, profited from the Roman occupation to line their own pockets. Many looked forward to the day when they would be delivered, when they would be free. Like Simeon, who was in the temple when Jesus' parents came to present their baby, they were 'waiting for Israel to be saved'.

So Jesus had to be careful to play down any claim to be the promised Messiah, the deliverer, for fear of raising people's hopes that he would lead a revolt against the Romans. The spirit of

The Jewish synagogue at Capernaum was sponsored by the local god-fearing Roman centurion: these ruins are of a slightly later building, probably on the same site and in the same style.

resistance was strongest among the Zealots (a guerilla group): and it was this spirit that led eventually to the disastrous events of the Jewish War, and the destruction of Jerusalem in AD 70.

But the time when the Jewish temple was destroyed and the Jewish nation scattered was also a time of a new beginning. After the death and resurrection of Jesus, it was made plain to his followers that the new kingdom was not just for the Jews but for all who believed in him. It offered a completely new start, not just for the Jewish people but for all who were to enter into the promises given to Abraham, which were based on faith. It was to mean liberation from sin and guilt and from the petty-fogging legalism of the Jewish Law. Jew and non-Jew ('Gentile') alike could begin a new life, filled with God's Spirit. The dynamic of this message was to turn the Empire upside down, and change the world.

A       B       C     *Mt Hermon*       D

•Tyre

**ISRAEL IN THE NEW TESTAMENT**

1

•Caesarea
Philippi

ITURAEA

TRACHONITIS

2

•Ptolemais

**Chorazin**
**Capernaum**    •**Bethsaida**
**Gennesaret**
**Cana**   **Magdala**   *Lake Galilee*
•**Sepphoris**   **2**    •**Tiberias**

3

**Nazareth**

GALILEE      •**Gadara**

•**Nain**        DECAPOLIS

•**Scythopolis**

*e Great Sea (Mediterranean)*

•**Caesarea**

•Aenon near Salim

**Samaria**•           •**Gerasa**

△   •**Sychar**
*Mt Gerizim*

**Antipatris**•

**Joppa**•       SAMARIA     PEREA

**1**

•**Lydda**

**2**

•**Jericho**

**Jerusalem**•    •**Bethany beyond**
     •**Bethphage**     **Jordan**
      •**Bethany**
•**Azotus**    •**Bethlehem**
     *Wilderness*
     *of Judea*

JUDEA

•**Machaerus**

•Gaza         *Dead Sea*

•**Masada**

NABATAEA

IDUMAEA

**1** Judea: Roman province
**2** Galilee and Perea:
    kingdom of Herod Antipas
**3** Tetrarchy of Philip

0   10   20   30   40 Km
0   5   10   15   20   25 M

1
2
3
4
5
6
7

**...AIN**
Paul hoped to bring the gospel here from Rome

**Rome**
Both Paul and Peter are thought to have ended their lives here, at the heart of the Roman Empire. Paul wrote to the Romans before visiting them, to set out the main facts of the gospel

**ITALY**

**GREECE**

**Corinth**
A cosmopolitan port. Paul's letters to the Corinthians show how the church was affected by the current problems of society, such as immorality, idol worship, mystery religions

**MALTA**
Paul was shipwrecked here while being taken to Rome as a prisoner

**Athens**
The cultural and religious heart of the ancient world and centre for many new cults; here Paul addressed the court convened to settle matters of religion

**CRETE**

# 15. The Outreach of the Church

The church grew first in Jerusalem under the apostles' leadership. Then the Jews stoned Stephen and persecuted the Christians.

Believers scattered all over Judea and Samaria; in towns and villages new Christian groups were founded (Acts 8). At this time (about AD 34) two important events occurred. Saul (Paul) the Pharisee, a fierce opponent of the new sect, was converted as he went to arrest believers in Damascus (Acts 9). In Caesarea Peter preached to a Roman centurion, Cornelius, who was baptized into the church – the first non-Jewish convert.

In Antioch, the capital of the province of Syria, Christians preached not only to Greek-speaking Jews ('hellenists') but to non-Jews ('Greeks') who had no connection with the Jewish religion. Many became believers; they were nicknamed 'Christians' (Acts 11:19-26). The church in Antioch sent out the first missionaries – Paul and Barnabas. They preached in Cyprus and what is now Turkey (Acts 13 – 14). Non-Jews as well as Jews became Christians. This led to a major problem. Could 'Gentiles' become Christians without first becoming Jews? The conference held at Jerusalem in about AD 48 decided that they could (Acts 15). It was a crucial step forward for the church.

Missionary activity increased. On his second journey Paul took the gospel into Europe (Acts 16), about AD 50. His third journey ended in his arrest, but he finally reached Rome in AD 62 and although he was a prisoner, he was able to preach freely (Acts 28). Many others were preaching the gospel and helping the churches. By AD 64, when the book of Acts ends, there were churches in all the main centres of the Empire, and from these the gospel was spreading out to surrounding areas.

**Alexandria**
Later a centre of Greek Christian thought

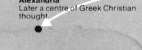

Paul first landed in Europe at the harbour of Neapolis, in northern Greece.

**Philippi**
The first church in 'Europe' was formed here as a result of the conversion of the jailer and his family. The letter to the Philippians was written to the church here

MACEDONIA

*Egnatian Way*
A main Roman road running from Dyrrachium (in modern Albania) to Byzantium

**Byzantium**

**Thessalonica**
Paul wrote to the Thessalonians to reassure them about the return of Christ

**Troas**
While staying here Paul and his companions were convinced that they should cross into Europe. Troas is the site of ancient Troy

**Colossae**
Paul wrote his letter to the Colossians to Christians in this hellenistic city, one of three in the area (Colossae, Laodicea, Hierapolis)

GALATIA
Paul wrote his letter to the Galatians to Christians in this area who were threatened by Jewish legalists

**Patmos**
While exiled here John wrote the book of Revelation to the Christians on the mainland who were suffering persecution.

**Ephesus**
A great hellenistic city and port; here was the great temple of Diana; the theatre where the crowd cried for Paul's blood; the 'hall of Tyrannus' where Paul taught for two years. The letter to the Ephesians was written to Christians in this district

**Pisidian Antioch**
Paul visited and re-visited the cities of Pisidia and Galatia, which had been influenced both by hellenistic culture, and by Jews who settled there, when speaking to God-fearers, he told them about Jesus; with pagans he started from God the Creator

**Tarsus**
Birthplace of Saul, who became known by his Roman name Paul

The gospel was taken east as far as India, according to traditions outside the New Testament

**Antioch**
A main centre of the church, where followers of Jesus were first called 'Christians'. Paul was sent out from here on his missionary journeys

CYPRUS
Birthplace of Barnabas, so a natural first place for Paul and Barnabas to visit on the first missionary journey

**Joppa**
Here Peter became convinced that the gospel was for non-Jews as well as Jews

**Damascus**
Paul was travelling here to suppress the Christians when he was converted by the risen Christ

**Jerusalem**
The church's outreach started when the disciples were given the Holy Spirit on the Day of Pentecost. Jerusalem remained a main centre of the church. The conference to decide how far non-Jews should keep the Jewish Law was held here in about AD 48

**Samaria**
The gospel was brought here from Jerusalem to a despised minority

Ephesus, a major city of Asia Minor.

# Paul's journeys

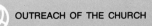

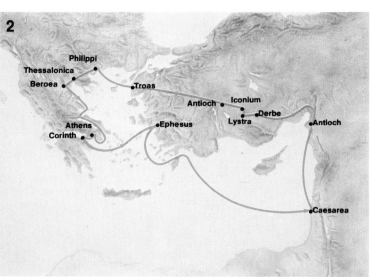

**2**

Philippi
Thessalonica
Beroea
Troas
Antioch
Iconium
Derbe
Lystra
Antioch
Athens
Ephesus
Corinth
Caesarea

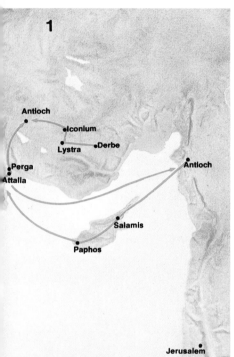

**1**

Antioch
Iconium
Lystra
Derbe
Perga
Attalia
Antioch
Salamis
Paphos
Jerusalem

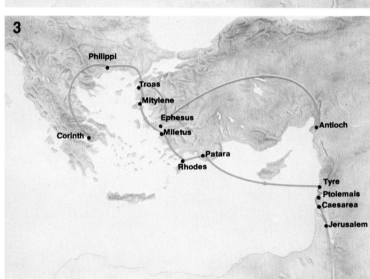

**3**

Philippi
Troas
Mitylene
Ephesus
Miletus
Corinth
Antioch
Patara
Rhodes
Tyre
Ptolemais
Caesarea
Jerusalem

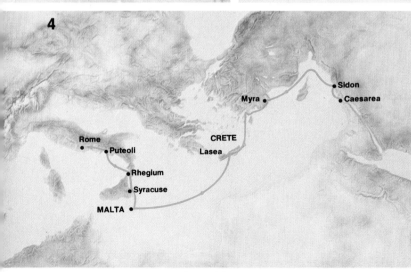

**4**

Sidon
Myra
Caesarea
Rome
Puteoli
CRETE
Lasea
Rhegium
Syracuse
MALTA

# The seven churches of Revelation

ASIA

Pergamum
Thyatira
Sardis
Philadelphia
Smyrna
Ephesus
Laodicea

# Places of the Bible

**Abana** Now called Barada, 'cool'. One of two rivers which flow through Damascus in Syria. When Elisha's servant told Naaman to bathe in the River Jordan and be healed, the Syrian general despised the muddy Jordan compared with the clear, fast-flowing waters of Abana and Pharpar.
2 Kings 5:12

**Abel-beth-maacah** A town in the north of Israel, near Lake Huleh, to which Joab pursued Sheba.

Houses cluster on the steep slope beneath the walls of the ancient temple area, Jerusalem.

Captured by Aramaeans of Damascus and recaptured more than once.
2 Samuel 20; 1 Kings 15:20; 2 Kings 15:29/*6; C1*

**Abel-meholah** The place to which the Midianites fled after Gideon's attack. The home-town of Elisha.
Judges 7:22; 1 Kings 19:16/*6; C4*

**Abilene** The region north-west of Damascus, governed by Lysanias.
Luke 3:1

**Accad** Name of a region and a city in ancient Babylonia, founded by Nimrod. See *Akkadians* and Map in Part 1: *Environment of the Bible,* under *The Babylonians.*
Genesis 10:10/*3*

**Achaia** The Roman province of southern Greece governed from Corinth.
Acts 18:12, etc./*13*

**Achor** 'Trouble Valley', near Jericho, where Achan was killed because he disobeyed God's command.
Joshua 7:24

**Adam** The place where the River Jordan was blocked, allowing the Israelites to cross into the Promised Land. In 1927 earth tremors caused the high clay banks to collapse at the same spot, and the Jordan was dammed for twenty-one hours.
Joshua 3:16/*6; C4*

**Admah** One of a group of five cities, of which Sodom and Gomorrah are best-known, now probably under the southern end of the Dead Sea. The kings of these cities formed an alliance and rebelled against four northern kings in Abraham's day. In the battle that followed, Abraham's nephew Lot was taken captive.
Genesis 10:19; 14:2

**Adramyttium** A port near Troy (Troas) on the west coast of what is now Turkey. A ship from Adramyttium took Paul and his fellow prisoners on the first stage of their journey to Rome.
Acts 27:2 / *15*

**Adullam** David, on the run from King Saul and fearing King Achish of Gath, took refuge in a 'cave' (probably a fort) near this town. His family and a group of 400 outlaws joined him in hiding. While he was there, three of David's bravest soldiers risked their lives to bring him water from the well at Bethlehem, which was held by the Philistines.
1 Samuel 22:1; 2 Samuel 23:13

**Aenon near Salim** The place where John the Baptist baptized his followers.
John 3:23 / *14; C3*

**Ahava** The name of a canal and a region in Babylonia where Ezra assembled the second party of returning Jewish exiles. Here they fasted and prayed for God's protection on their 900 mile/1,448 km journey to Jerusalem.
Ezra 8:15, 21, 31

**Ai** The name means 'the Ruin'. After capturing Jericho, Joshua sent a small force against nearby Ai – and was beaten. The reason was because Achan had defied God's command by taking spoil from Jericho. Achan was punished, and Joshua attacked Ai again. He lured the men of Ai out by pretending to run away, and a hidden ambush force moved in and set fire to the stronghold. See Part 2: *Archaeology and the Bible.*
Joshua 7 and 8 / *6; B4*

**Aijalon** An Amorite town belonging by right to the tribe of Dan, but given to the Levites. Much later King Rehoboam fortified the

Antioch in Syria, next in importance to Jerusalem as a centre for the early Christians. This building, part-way up the steep hillside which overlooks the busy modern city, is claimed as the site of the first church there.

city and kept stores and arms there.
Joshua 19:42; 21:24; Judges 1:35; 2 Chronicles 11:10 / *6; B5*

**Aijalon** A valley through which an important trade-route passed; near to the town of Aijalon. In this valley Joshua fought a great battle against the Amorites, and 'the sun stood still'.
Joshua 10 / *6; B5*

**Alexandria** A great Egyptian sea-port on the Nile Delta founded by Alexander the Great. The famous Pharos light-house tower stood at the harbour entrance. Alexandria was the capital of Egypt under the Ptolemies, and remained a great centre of learning and trade.

In Roman times grain-ships loaded up at Alexandria so that the people of Rome could have cheap bread. The city had a 'museum' of arts and sciences and a famous library containing thousands of papyrus scrolls. There was a strong Jewish community, and it was here that the Old Testament was translated into Greek – the Septuagint version. Apollos, who became an important teacher in the early church, came from Alexandria.
Acts 6:9; 18:24; 27:6; 28:11 / *11*

**Ammon** A state on the east of the Jordan whose capital was Rabbah (modern Amman). See *Rabbah; Ammonites* and Map in Part 1: *Environment of the Bible.* / *6; C4*

**Amphipolis** A town on Paul's route through northern Greece on his second missionary journey.
Acts 17:1 / *15*

**Anathoth** A town 3 miles/4km north of Jerusalem belonging to the Levites. The birthplace of Jeremiah.
Joshua 21:18; Jeremiah 1:1 / *6; B5*

**Antioch ('Pisidian')** A town in the heart of Asia Minor (present-day Turkey) visited by Paul and Barnabas on their first missionary journey. They preached first in the synagogue, but when non-Jews responded to Paul's message the Jews stirred up trouble and threw Paul and Barnabas out of the city. Two or three years later, Paul visited Antioch again, on his second missionary journey, to encourage the Christians in their new faith.
Acts 13:14–52 / *15*

**Antioch in Syria** (modern Antakya, on the Syrian border of Turkey). The most famous of sixteen cities with this name, founded by one of Alexander's generals in honour of his father. Antioch, on the River Orontes, had its own sea-port. Under the Romans it became the capital of the province of Syria and third largest city of the Empire, renowned for its culture. It had a large Jewish community. After the death of Stephen, persecuted Christians fled the 300 miles/483 km from Jerusalem to Antioch.

This was the start of one of the largest and most active of the early Christian churches. Many local people were converted, including a large number of Greeks, and it was here that they were first called 'Christians'.

Barnabas, who had been sent from Jerusalem to find out what was happening, set off to find Paul and ask him to help teach the new converts. They taught together in Antioch for over a year. Some time later the church at Antioch sent Paul and Barnabas out to teach in Cyprus and beyond. Antioch remained Paul's base, and for a long time the church there was second only to Jerusalem. The ancient city was levelled by an earthquake in AD 526.
Acts 11:19–26; 13:1; 15:35/*13*

**Antipatris** A town rebuilt by King Herod and named in honour of his father, Antipater. When Paul's life was threatened he was taken under escort from Jerusalem to Caesarea on the coast. On the way they spent the night at Antipatris.
Acts 23:31/*14*

**Aphek** The Philistines camped at Aphek before the battle in which they captured the Covenant Box (ark) from the Israelites. Eli's sons took the ark to the Israelite camp. Both were killed in the battle, and Eli fell to his death when he heard the news. Much later Aphek became Antipatris.
1 Samuel 4:1/*6; B4*

**Ar** Capital of Moab, on the River Arnon. During their time in the desert after leaving Egypt the Israelites were told to leave this city in peace. God had given it to the Moabites, Lot's descendants.
Numbers 21:15; Deuteronomy 2:9; Isaiah 15:1/*6; C6*

**Arabah** The rift valley of the River Jordan, stretching from Lake Galilee in the north to the Dead Sea in the south and continuing on to the Gulf of Aqaba. The 'Sea of Arabah' is the Dead Sea./*1*

**Arad** A Canaanite town in the Negev defeated by Joshua. See Part 2: *Archaeology and the Bible* under *Archaeology and Israelite Religion.*
Joshua 12:14/*6; B6*

**Aram** A group name for various states in southern Syria, especially Damascus. See *Aramaeans* and Map in Part 1: *Environment of the Bible.*

**Ararat** The mountain country where Noah's ark came to rest when the flood waters drained away. The area, called Urartu in Assyrian inscriptions, is Armenia, on the borders of present-day Turkey and Russia. Mount Ararat itself is an extinct volcano nearly 17,000ft/5,214m high.
Genesis 8:4; Jeremiah 51:27/*3*

The famous centuries-old city of Athens. In the foreground is the 'agora', the public meeting-place and city-centre of Athens in New Testament times. On the left is the reconstructed stoa, with its colonnades; the Parthenon, on the Acropolis, dominates the centre; and to the right is Mars Hill

**Areopagus** 'Mars hill', north-west of the acropolis in Athens, from which the Council of the Areopagus (which originally met there) took its name.
Acts 17

**Argob** Part of the kingdom of Og in Bashan, east of the Jordan. It was given to the half tribe of Manasseh, and was a fertile region with many strong towns.
Deuteronomy 3; 1 Kings 4/*6; D2*

**Arimathea** The home of Joseph, a secret disciple of Jesus, in whose new rock-tomb the body of Jesus was placed after he was crucified.
Matthew 27:57; Mark 15:43

**Armaggedon** See *Megiddo.*

**Arnon** A river which flows into the Dead Sea from the east (now Wadi Mujib). It formed the border between the Amorites and Moabites. The invading Hebrews defeated the Amorites and their land was settled by the tribe of Reuben. The River Arnon remained the southern border.
Numbers 21:13ff.; Isaiah 16:2/*1*

**Aroer** A town on the north bank of the River Arnon, east of Jordan. The southern limit of the Amorite kingdom and later of the tribe of Reuben. Under Moabite rule from the time of Jehu to Jeremiah's day. Also the name of a town in the Negev, south of Beersheba.
Deuteronomy 2:36, etc.; 2 Kings 10:33/*6; C6*

**Ashdod** One of five Philistine strongholds in Old Testament times. When the Philistines captured the Covenant Box (ark) they took it to the temple of their god Dagon at Ashdod. Next morning they discovered the statue of Dagon flat on its face; the following day it was broken in pieces. Ashdod fell to King Uzziah of Judah in Isaiah's time. In New Testament times the city (called Azotus) was restored by King Herod.
1 Samuel 5; 2 Chronicles 26:6; Isaiah 20:1, etc.; Acts 8:40/*6; A5*

**Ashkelon** An ancient city on the coast of Israel, between Jaffa and Gaza. It became one of the main strongholds of the Philistines. Samson made a raid on Ashkelon,

killing thirty men to pay what he owed in a bet. In the centuries that followed, Ashkelon was ruled in turn by Assyria, Babylonia and Tyre. In New Testament times Herod the Great was born at Ashkelon.
Judges 1:18; 14:19; 1 Samuel 6:17; Jeremiah 47:5–7, etc. /6; A5

**Ashtaroth/Ashteroth-karnaim** A city east of the Jordan, named after the Canaanite mother-goddess. It was captured by Chedorlaomer in Abraham's time and later became a capital of King Og of Bashan. One of the cities given to the Levites.
Genesis 14:5; Deuteronomy 1:4; 1 Chronicles 6:71 /6; D2

**Asia** The western part of Asia Minor (modern Turkey) including a number of important Greek city-states. Later the Roman province of Asia, including the whole west coast, whose most important city was Ephesus. Much of Paul's missionary work took place in this region.
Acts 2:9; 19:10; Revelation 1:4,11 /15

**Assos** The sea-port on the west coast of modern Turkey from which Paul set out on his last journey to Jerusalem.
Acts 20:13 /15

**Assyria** An important country in north Mesopotamia. Assyria was a great power from the ninth to the seventh century BC. See *The Assyrians* and Map in Part 1: *Environment of the Bible.*

**Ataroth** A town east of the Jordan, given to the tribe of Reuben.
Numbers 32:3,34 /6; C5

**Athens** The capital of modern Greece which first became important in the sixth century BC. The city was at the height of its greatness in the fifth century BC when its most famous public buildings, including the Parthenon, were built. Athens was then a model democracy and centre of the arts, attracting playwrights, historians, philosophers and scientists from all over Greece. In 86 BC the city was besieged and stripped by the Romans.
Although it lost its power and wealth as a centre of trade Athens still had a great name for learning

in the mid-50s AD when Paul arrived on his second missionary journey, preaching about Jesus and the resurrection. The Athenians loved a discussion and called him to speak before their council. Paul used their altar, dedicated 'To an Unknown God', as his starting-point. He spoke about the God who made the world and is near to each one of us. (Picture page 259.)
Acts 17:15–34 /13

**Attalia** Modern Antalya, a port on the south coast of Turkey, used by Paul on his first missionary journey.
Acts 14:25 /15

**Azekah** The town to which Joshua pursued the Amorites; later a fortified border city of Judah.
Joshua 10:10; Jeremiah 34:7

**Babel** (predecessor of ancient Babylon) After the flood, when people still spoke one language, they planned to build a city on the plain of Shinar (Sumer) in the

The harbour at Antalya (New Testament Attalia) where Paul took ship after preaching in the inland cities of what is now southern Turkey.

land of the two rivers (Mesopotamia) – and a tower that would reach to heaven. God saw their pride and brought the work to a standstill by confusing their language, so that they could not understand one another.
Genesis 10:10; 11:1–9

**Babylon** A city on the River Euphrates, 50 miles/80 km south of modern Baghdad. Babylon was founded by Nimrod 'the mighty hunter'. It later became the capital of Babylonia and the Babylonian Empire. About 1750 BC, Hammurabi, one of the early kings of Babylon, wrote down on stone a great code of laws which it is interesting to compare with the later laws of Moses.
After the defeat of Assyria in 612 BC Babylon became capital of a powerful empire extending from the Persian Gulf to the Mediterranean. In 597 and 586 BC King Nebuchadnezzar of Babylon conquered rebellious Jerusalem. On each occasion, many of the people of Judah were taken into exile to Babylon – among them the prophets Ezekiel and Daniel.
The city covered a huge area on

both banks of the Euphrates. Both inner and outer city were protected by double brick walls 11-25ft/3-7m thick. Eight great gates led to the inner city, and there were fifty temples. The 'hanging gardens' of Babylon was one of the wonders of the ancient world. These were terraces on different levels laid out with palms and many other trees and plants, providing colour and shade in a flat land.

In 539 BC the Persians, under Cyrus, took the city. Herodotus, the Greek historian, says they diverted the River Euphrates and marched along the dried-up river bed to enter the city. From that time on, Babylon declined. Nothing remains today but a series of widely scattered mounds, for the archaeologists to work on. See Part 1: *Environment of the Bible* under *The Babylonians*.
Genesis 10:10; 2 Kings 24:1; 25:7–13; Isaiah 14:1–23; Daniel 1 – 6/*3*

**Bashan** A fertile region east of Lake Galilee, famous for its cattle, sheep and strong oak trees. On their way from Egypt to Canaan the Israelites defeated King Og of Bashan, and his land was given to the tribe of Manasseh.
Deuteronomy 3; Psalm 22:12; Isaiah 2:13/*6; C2*

**Beersheba** The southernmost town to belong to the Israelites, on the edge of the Negev Desert, and on the trade route to Egypt. The well (*be'er*) which gave the town its name was dug by Abraham. Hagar came near to death in the desert of Beersheba. It was from this place that Abraham set out to offer up Isaac. Isaac himself was living here when Jacob left for Harran. Beersheba is also mentioned in connection with Elijah and Amos. The phrase 'from Dan to Beersheba' became a common way to speak of the whole land, from north to south. See Part 2: *Archaeology and the Bible.*
Genesis 21:14, 30–32; 26:23–33; 1 Kings 19:3; Amos 5:5/*6; A6*

**Beroea** A town in northern Greece (Macedonia), 50 miles/80km from Thessalonica. Paul preached here on his second missionary journey. The Beroeans

Bethany. He ascended to heaven from a place nearby.
Matthew 26:6–13; Luke 10:38–42; 24:50; John 11; 12:1–9 /*14; B5*

**Bethel** A place 12 miles/19km north of Jerusalem where Jacob dreamed of a staircase from heaven to earth. God promised to protect him, and said he would give the land to Jacob's descendants. Jacob called the place 'Bethel' (house of God). Centuries later, when the Israelites invaded Canaan, they captured Bethel and settled there.

When the kingdoms of Israel and Judah split up, King Jeroboam of Israel set up an altar and golden calf at Bethel, so that people could worship there instead of at Jerusalem. The prophets condemned this, and when the Israelites were taken into exile Bethel was settled by Assyrians. When the exiles returned, some of them lived in Bethel.
Genesis 28:10–22; Judges 1:22–26; 20:18; Kings 12:26–30;

A lion relief from the walls of Babylon.

welcomed him because they studied the Scriptures. But Jews from Thessalonica stirred up the mob against him and he had to leave. But Silas and Timothy stayed behind to teach the Beroeans more about the Christian faith.
Acts 17:10–15; 20:4/*15*

**Bethany** A village about 2 miles/3km from Jerusalem on the far side of the Mount of Olives, and on the road to Jericho. Mary, Martha and Lazarus lived here, and Jesus stayed with them when he visited Jerusalem. Jesus raised Lazarus from the grave at

2 Kings 2; 17:28; Nehemiah 11:31/*6; B4*

**Bethesda/Bethzatha** A large pool in Jerusalem. At the time of Jesus it was sheltered by five porches, and it is probably the five-porched pool that has been unearthed by archaeologists in the north-east of the city. The pool was fed by a spring which bubbled up from time to time. Many sick people gathered there, hoping to be healed if they were first into the water after this bubbling. It was here that Jesus healed a man who had been ill for thirty-eight years.
John 5:1–15

**Beth-horon (Upper and Lower)**
These two towns controlled the Valley of Aijalon and the ancient trade-route which passed through it. Many armies took this route in Bible times. Here Joshua pursued the Amorite kings who had attacked the town of Gibeon. Philistines, Egyptians and Syrians also came here.
Joshua 16:3–5; 10:10; 1 Samuel 13:18/*6; B4*

**Bethlehem** The city of David, 5 miles/8km south-west of Jerusalem, in the Judean hills. Rachel,

wife of Jacob, was buried nearby. Ruth and Naomi settled here. Bethlehem was David's birth-place, and the place where the prophet Samuel chose him as the future king, to succeed Saul. The prophet Micah foretold the birth of the Messiah at Bethlehem, although it was only a small town.
Centuries later the Roman census brought Mary and Joseph to Bethlehem. Shepherds and wise men came to kneel before their baby, Jesus – born in a stable in the 'city of David'. Not long after, jealous King Herod gave orders to kill all the boys in Bethlehem under two years old.
Genesis 35:19; Ruth; 1 Samuel 16; Micah 5:2; Matthew 2; Luke 2/*14; B5*

**Bethphage** A village near Bethany, on or near the Mount of Olives, on the east side of Jerusalem. When Jesus came here on his last journey to Jerusalem,

he sent two disciples to a nearby village to fetch the young colt on which he rode in triumph into the city.
Matthew 21:1; Mark 11:1; Luke 19:29/*14; B5*

**Bethsaida** A fishing town on the north shore of Lake Galilee, near the River Jordan. The home of Jesus' disciples, Philip, Andrew and Peter. Jesus restored the sight of a blind man at Bethsaida, and warned the people of God's judgement. Although they saw his miracles they would not change their ways.
John 1:44; Mark 8:22; Matthew 11:21/*14; C2*

An aerial view of the town of Bethlehem, birthplace of Jesus and of David.

**Beth-shan** A very ancient city in northern Palestine where the Valley of Jezreel slopes down to the west bank of the River Jordan. The Israelites failed to drive the Canaanites out of this district. After Saul and Jonathan were killed by the Philistines on Mt Gilboa, their bodies were fixed on the walls of Beth-shan, but later rescued and buried by men from Jabesh-gilead. In New Testament times Beth-shan was known by the Greek name Scythopolis, and became one of the cities of the Decapolis, the only one west of the Jordan (see *Decapolis*). The modern town of Beisan stands close to the mound of the old site.
Joshua 17:11,16; Judges 1:27; 1 Samuel 31:10–13; 2 Samuel 21:12; 1 Kings 4:12/*6; C3*

**Beth-shemesh** A town about 12 miles/19km west of Jerusalem,

given to the priests. It was near the borders of the Philistines. When the Covenant Box (ark) was returned by the Philistines, it came to Beth-shemesh. But some of the people here were punished for not treating it with respect. Later Jehoash, king of the northern kingdom of Israel, defeated and captured Amaziah, king of Judah, at Beth-shemesh.
Joshua 21:16; 1 Samuel 6:9–21; 1 Kings 4:9; 2 Kings 14:11–13 /*6; B5*

**Beth-zur** A city of Judah, 4 miles/6km north of Hebron. Beth-zur was settled by the family of Caleb. Later it was one of fifteen cities fortified by King Rehoboam. Men from here helped to rebuild Jerusalem under Nehemiah's leadership. The place stood on one of the highest hill-tops in the land, and was the scene of one of the great Jewish victories in the Maccabean revolt (*1 Maccabees* 4:26–35).
Joshua 15:58; 1 Chronicles 2:45; 2 Chronicles 11:7; Nehemiah 3:16/*6; B6*

**Bithynia** A Roman province in the north-west of Asia Minor (Turkey). Paul was forbidden 'by the Holy Spirit' to preach here. Yet Bithynia was not forgotten. Peter sent his first letter to Christian believers living in Bithynia, among other places. We know that this area soon became a strong centre of Christianity, for early in the second century the Roman governor Pliny wrote to the Emperor Trajan about the Christians there (see Part 5).
Acts 16:7; 1 Peter 1:1/*13*

**Bozrah** An ancient city in Edom, south-east of the Dead Sea, about 80 miles/128km south of modern Amman in Jordan. The prophets foretold that Bozrah would be utterly destroyed.
Genesis 36:33; 1 Chronicles 1:44; Isaiah 34:6; 63:1; Jeremiah 49:13, 22; Amos 1:12/*6; C5*

**Caesarea** A Mediterranean port built by Herod the Great. He named the town after the Roman Emperor Augustus Caesar. Statues of the Emperor stood in a huge temple dedicated to him and to Rome. Traders on their way from Tyre to Egypt passed through Caesarea. So it was a centre of inland as well as seatrade.

Caesarea was the home town of Philip the evangelist. It was also the home of Cornelius, the Roman centurion who sent for Peter, asking him to explain God's message. It was here that Peter learned that 'the Good News of peace through Jesus Christ' was for non-Jews as well as Jews.

Paul several times used the port on his travels. The Roman governors lived here, rather than at Jerusalem, so it was here that Paul was taken for trial before Felix after his arrest. He spent two further years in prison here. From Caesarea he sailed for Rome after his appeal to Caesar.
Acts 8:40; 21:8; 10; 11; 9:30; 18:22; 23:33 – 26:32/ *14; A3*

**Caesarea Philippi** A town at the foot of Mt Hermon and close to the main source of the River Jordan. Herod the Great built a marble temple here to Augustus Caesar. And one of his sons, Philip, changed the town's name from Paneas to Caesarea. It was known as Philip's Caesarea to distinguish it from the port.

Jesus had taken his disciples to this part of the country when he asked them, 'Who do you say I am?' The answer came from Peter: 'You are the Messiah, the Son of the living God.'
Matthew 16:13–16/ *14; C1*

**Calah** A very ancient city of Mesopotamia on the River Tigris, later a leading city of the Assyrian Empire. Excavations at the site, now Nimrud in Iraq, have unearthed inscriptions and ivory-carvings which throw light on the times of the kings of Israel.
Genesis 10:11–12/ *9*

**Cana** The village in Galilee where Jesus turned the water into wine at a wedding. During another visit to Cana, Jesus healed the son of an official from Capernaum. Nathanael, one of Jesus' twelve disciples, came from Cana.
John 2:1–12; 4:46–53; 21–2 / *14; B2*

**Canaan** The land promised by God to the Israelites. See *Canaanites* in Part 1: *Environment of the Bible./3*

**Capernaum** An important town on the north-west shore of Lake Galilee at the time of Jesus. It was Jesus' base while he was teaching in Galilee. Levi (Matthew) the tax-

collector lived at Capernaum. So too did a Roman army officer whose servant Jesus healed. There may have been an army post here. Many of Jesus' miracles took place at Capernaum, including the healing of Peter's mother-in-law. Jesus also taught in the local synagogue. But despite all this, the people of the town did not believe God's message, and Jesus had to warn them of coming judgement.
Mark 1:21–34; 2:1–17;
Luke 7:1–10; 10:13–16, etc.
/ *14; C2*

**Cappadocia** A Roman province in the east of Asia Minor (Turkey).

Cana, the town in the hills of Galilee where Jesus went to a wedding, and turned water into wine.

There were Jews from Cappadocia among those who heard Peter in Jerusalem on the Day of Pentecost. Later the Christians in Cappadocia were among those to whom Peter sent his first letter.
Acts 2:9; 1 Peter 1:1/ *13*

**Carchemish** An important Hittite city from early times, on the River Euphrates. The ruins now lie on the border between Turkey and Syria. When the Egyptian Pharaoh (king) Neco went to attack Carchemish, Josiah, the king of Judah, made a needless attempt to oppose him, and was defeated and killed in the plain of Megiddo. In 605 BC Neco himself was defeated at Carchemish by Nebuchadnezzar, king of Babylon.
2 Chronicles 35:20; Isaiah 10:9; Jeremiah 46:2/ *9*

**Carmel** A range of hills which juts into the Mediterranean Sea close to the modern port of Haifa. The ancient city of Megiddo guarded one of the main passes through the hills some miles inland. It was on Mt Carmel (1,740ft/535m at the highest point) that Elijah, God's prophet, challenged the prophets of Baal to a contest. Elisha, who followed Elijah as prophet, also seems to have made a base there.
1 Kings 18:19–46; 2 Kings 2:25; 4:25/ *6; B3*

**Cenchreae** The eastern port of Corinth in southern Greece, from which Paul sailed to Ephesus.
Acts 18:8; Romans 16:1/ *15*

**Chaldea** South Babylonia; Abraham's family home. See Chaldeans and Map in Part 1: *Environment of the Bible*

**Chebar** A canal running from the River Euphrates in Babylonia (S.Iraq). It was by the Chebar that the prophet Ezekiel, in exile with the Jews in Babylonia, saw some of his great visions of God.
Ezekiel 1; 3; 10; 43

**Cherith** A desert stream east of the Jordan. Here God provided food and water for Elijah during years of drought and famine, until the stream itself dried up. We do not know exactly where the Cherith was.
1 Kings 17:3–7

**Chinnereth** The Old Testament name for Lake Galilee, from a

The temple of Apollo at Corinth, with the Acro-corinth behind. In ancient times the temple of Aphrodite, goddess of love, dominated the town from this height.

place on its western shore. The name is used in descriptions of the boundaries of lands belonging to the tribes of Israel, and of nearby kingdoms. See *Galilee*.
Numbers 34:11; Deuteronomy 3:17; Joshua 11:2, etc.; 1 Kings 15:20

**Chorazin** A town where Jesus taught, near Capernaum, on a hill above Lake Galilee. Jesus was deeply troubled that these places which heard his teaching did not show any change of heart and life as a result. The site of Chorazin is now a deserted ruin.
Matthew 11:21; Luke 10:13
/*14; C2*

**Cilicia** A region in south Asia Minor (modern Turkey) which became a province of the Roman Empire in 103 BC. Tarsus, where Paul was born, was the chief town of Cilicia. Behind it, running north-east, lay the wild Taurus

mountains, cut through by an impressive pass known as the Cilician Gates.
Acts 21:39; 22:3; 23:34/*13*

**Colossae** A town in the Lycus Valley, in the Roman province of Asia (now south-west Turkey). It stood just a few miles from Laodicea, on the main road east from Ephesus. The Christian message probably reached Colossae when Paul was staying at Ephesus, though he himself never went there. Paul wrote a letter (Colossians) to the church there.
Colossians 1:2/*15*

**Corinth** An old Greek city destroyed by the Romans in 146 BC and rebuilt by them a hundred years later. Corinth stood on the narrow neck of land connecting mainland Greece with the southern peninsula, between the Aegean and Adriatic seas. It was a good position for trade.

The town attracted people of many nationalities. It was dominated by the 'Acro-corinth', the steep rock on which the acropolis and a temple to Aphrodite (goddess of love) was built. Temple prostitutes and a large 'floating' population helped to give Corinth a very bad name for all kinds of immoral behaviour.

Paul stayed in Corinth for eighteen months, on his second missionary journey. During that time he founded a church to which he later wrote at least two letters now in the New Testament (1 and 2 Corinthians).
Acts 18/*15*

**Crete** A mountainous island in the eastern Mediterranean Sea. The 'Cherethites', who formed part of King David's bodyguard, probably came from Crete. Much earlier, from before 2000 BC until after 1400 BC, the Minoan civilization flourished on the island. It was a home of the Philistines.

In the New Testament, men from Crete were in Jerusalem on the Day of Pentecost. Paul's ship called at the island on its way to Rome. At some stage he had visited Crete and left Titus there to help the newly-formed church. See *Philistines* in Part 1: *Environment of the Bible*.
Genesis 10:14; Deuteronomy 2:23; Jeremiah 47:4; Amos 9:7; Acts 2:11; 28:7–14; Titus 1:5, 12–13/*3*

**Cush** A land in Africa (Sudan) named after the grandson of Noah. The English versions sometimes translate the name as Ethiopia. See Part 1: *Environment of the Bible*.
Genesis 10:6–8; Isaiah 11:11; 18:11

**Cyprus** A large island in the eastern Mediterranean Sea. In the Old Testament 'Elishah' may refer to Cyprus, and 'Kittim' to Cypriots.

In the New Testament Cyprus features as the home of Barnabas. It was the first place Paul and Barnabas visited when they set out to take the good news of Jesus to the non-Jewish world. Here they met the governor, Sergius Paulus, and his magician friend. Barnabas later returned to Cyprus with Mark.
Acts 4:36; 13:4–12; 15:39; 27:4/*3*

**Cyrene** A Greek city on the north coast of Africa, in modern Libya. A man from Cyrene, Simon, was forced to carry Jesus' cross. Jews from Cyrene were among those present in Jerusalem on the Day of Pentecost. Other Cyrenians became involved in the earliest mission to non-Jews, at Antioch.
Matthew 27:32; Mark 15:21; Acts 2:10; 6:9; 11:20; 13:1/*13*

**Dalmatia** A Roman province on the east coast of the Adriatic Sea, along the coast of modern Yugoslavia. Paul's second letter to Timothy shows him almost alone at the end of his life. His friends have left him for various reasons. Titus has gone to Dalmatia.
2 Timothy 4:10/*13*

**Damascus** The capital of Syria (see *Aramaeans* in Part 1: *Environment of the Bible*). Damascus was already well known in Abraham's day, and is often mentioned in the Old Testament. King David captured the city, but it soon regained its independence. Damascus was the home of Naaman, who came to the prophet Elisha for healing. The prophet later went to Damascus to advise on the king's health.

Isaiah predicted the destruction of Damascus. And after a series of attacks the Assyrians captured the city in 732 BC, carried away its treasures and many of its people, and reduced its power. From 64 BC to AD 33 Damascus was a Roman city.

'Straight Street' in Damascus, the place where Paul recovered his sight, is today lined with small shops selling goods of all kinds. Damascus was an important city and centre of trade in Old as well as New Testament times. The inset picture shows a local weaver at his loom.

Paul was on his way to Damascus to persecute the Christians when he met with Jesus himself, and the whole direction of his life was changed. He had to escape from the city later, when the Jews persecuted him.
Genesis 14:15; 15:2; 2 Samuel 8:5; 1 Kings 20:34; 2 Kings 5; 8:7–15; Isaiah 17; Acts 9/*3*

**Dan** The land belonging to the tribe of Dan, and a town (Laish) in the far north of Israel. Dan was the northernmost city of Israel, and the expression 'from Dan to Beersheba' meant 'from one end of the land to the other'. When the kingdom was divided, Jeroboam I tried to keep the loyalty of the northern tribes by giving them two golden calves to worship: one was at Dan.
Joshua 19: 40–48;
1 Kings 12:25–30/*6; C1*

**Dead Sea** See *Salt Sea* and *Arabah.*

**Decapolis (the Ten Towns)** An association of ten Greek towns gave this region its name. The Decapolis was an area south of Lake Galilee, mostly east of the River Jordan. Many of the people living there were non-Jews, but they joined the crowds that followed Jesus. Jewish Christians fled to Pella, one of these towns, before the war with the Romans in AD 70.
Matthew 4:25; Mark 5:1–20; 7:31–37/*14; C3*

**Dedan** See *Dedan* in Part 1: *Environment of the Bible.*

**Derbe** A city in Lycaonia, in southern Asia Minor (modern Turkey), where Paul preached on his first and second journeys.
Acts 14:20–21; 16:1/*15*

**Dibon** A Moabite town east of the Dead Sea and 4 miles/5.5km north of the River Arnon. The Israelites captured it at the time of their entry into Canaan. It was given to the tribes of Gad and Reuben, but changed hands several times in the course of its history.
Numbers 21:30; 32:34;
Isaiah 15:2/*6; C6*

**Dor** A Canaanite town. Dor joined the northern alliance of kings who fought against Joshua and lost. The town was given to the tribe of Manasseh who failed to drive out its inhabitants.
Joshua 11:1–15; Judges 1:27; 1 Kings 4:11/6; B3

**Dothan** A town on the route from Beth-shan and Gilead to Egypt. Here Joseph's brothers sold him to the Ishmaelite traders. At Dothan, Elisha was rescued from the surrounding Syrian army.
Genesis 37:17–28; 2 Kings 6 /6; B3

**Ebal** A rocky mountain in Samaria, opposite the wooded height of Mt Gerizim, close to ancient Shechem and modern Nablus. Here Joshua carried out a command given him by Moses before the conquest of the land. He built an altar on Mt Ebal and gave the people a choice – to obey God and enjoy his blessing, or to disobey and be punished. Some of the people stood on Mt Ebal, whose bare, scorched height represented God's curse, and others on Mt Gerizim.
Deuteronomy 11:29; 27; Joshua 8:30, 33/6; B4

Ephesus, Turkey. The Arcadian Way, the Roman street leading to the theatre. The inset picture gives a performer's view of the theatre, as he made his entrance into the arena.

**Eden** The garden God made, in the beginning, as a place for his people to live in. After they had disobeyed him, God sent Adam and Eve out of the Garden of Eden. Two of the rivers in it were the Tigris and the Euphrates.
Genesis 2:8–14

**Edom** The mountainous land south of the Dead Sea where Esau's descendants settled. See *Edomites* and Map in Part 1: *Environment of the Bible.*

**Edrei** The site of a battle where the Israelites destroyed the army of Og, king of Bashan, who fought them before they entered the Promised Land. Edrei is the modern Der'a, on the Syrian frontier with Jordan.
Numbers 21:33; Deuteronomy 1:4; 3:1, 10; Joshua 12:4; 13:12, 31/6; D3

**Eglon** One of a group of Amorite cities conquered by Joshua in his first vigorous campaign. It was probably Tell el-Hesi near Lachish, in the Shephelah, the low hillish, in the Shephelah, the low hill-country west of Jerusalem. See Part 2: *Archaeology and the Bible.*
Joshua 10; 12:12; 15:39/6; A6

**Egypt** See *Egyptians* in Part 1: *Environment of the Bible.*

**Ekron** One of the five main cities of the Philistines. It was given to the tribe of Judah in the early years of conquest. But the Philistines on the coastal plain were too strong for them to keep it. When the Philistines defeated Israel and captured the Covenant Box (ark), plague broke out in each of the Philistine cities to which the ark was taken. When the plague reached Ekron, the Philistines finally decided to send the ark back to the Israelites. Ekron remained a Philistine city. When King Ahaziah turned away from the God of Israel, he sent to consult Baal-zebub, the god of Ekron. 'Beelzebub' was regarded in New Testament times as the prince of evil spirits.
Joshua 15:11, 45–46; Judges 1:18; 1 Samuel 5:10–6:17; 7:14;

17:52; 2 Kings 1:3–6;
Amos 1:8, etc./6; A5

**Elah** A valley south-west of Jerusalem. The Philistines marched through the Valley of Elah to invade the land of Israel. Here David fought the Philistine champion Goliath.
1 Samuel 17:2

**Elam** The country east of Babylonia whose capital was Susa. See *Elamites* in Part 1: *Environment of the Bible.*/3

**Elath/Ezion-geber** A settlement (later a town) at the head of the Gulf of Aqaba on the Red Sea. The Israelites camped there on their way from Egypt to Canaan. King Solomon based a Red Sea trading fleet there. King Jehoshaphat later tried to revive this, but his ships were wrecked. The town eventually came under Edomite control.
Numbers 33:35–36;
Deuteronomy 2:8;
1 Kings 9:26–27; 22:48;
2 Kings 16:6/5

**Emmaus** A village within 8 miles/13km of Jerusalem. It was probably modern El-Qubeibeh. On the day of his resurrection Jesus appeared to two of his followers who were on their way to Emmaus.
Luke 24:13/14; B5

**Endor** A place in northern Israel, near Mt Tabor. King Saul made a secret journey to Endor on the night before his last battle. He wanted to ask the witch (or medium) there to call up the spirit of the dead prophet Samuel, to advise him. Saul and his son Jonathan were killed next day in

The River Euphrates as it flows through the parched lands of Syria on its way to Babylonia and the Persian Gulf.

the disastrous defeat at nearby Mt Gilboa.
1 Samuel 28/6; B3

**Engedi** A spring to the west of the Dead Sea where David hid out.
Joshua 15:62; 1 Samuel 23:29, etc./6; B6

**En-rogel** A well on the south side of Jerusalem, near where the Hinnom Valley joins the Kidron Valley. Adonijah, one of King David's sons, had himself anointed king here before his father's death. He was trying to prevent the kingdom from going to Solomon.
1 Kings 1:9

**Ephesus** The most important city in the Roman province of Asia (western Turkey). Ephesus was a bridgehead between East and West. It stood at the end of one of the great caravan trade routes through Asia, at the mouth of the Cayster River. By Paul's day the harbour was beginning to silt up. But the city was magnificent, with streets paved in marble, baths, libraries, a market-place and theatre seating more than 25,000 people. The temple to Diana at Ephesus was one of the seven wonders of the ancient world, four times the size of the Parthenon at Athens.

There had been a settlement at Ephesus since before the twelfth century BC. But by New Testament times the population had grown to something like a third of a million, including a great many Jews.

Ephesus soon became an

important centre for the early Christians, too. Paul made a brief visit on his second missionary journey, and his friends Aquila and Prisca stayed on there. On his third journey he spent over two years at Ephesus, and the Christian message spread widely throughout the province. Sales of silver images of Diana began to fall off. People's incomes were threatened and there was a riot.

Paul wrote his letters to Corinth from Ephesus. And some of his letters from prison (Philippians, etc.) may have been written from Ephesus. Timothy stayed behind to help the church when Paul left. Paul later wrote a letter to the Christians at Ephesus. One of the letters to the seven churches in Revelation was also addressed to them.

There is a tradition that Ephesus became the home of the apostle John.
Acts 18:19; 19; 20:17;
1 Corinthians 15:32; 16:8–9;
Ephesians 1:1; 1 Timothy 1:3;
Revelation 2:1–7/13

**Ephraim** The land belonging to the tribe of Ephraim.
Joshua 16:4–10, etc./5

**Ephrathah** Another name for Bethlehem.

**Erech** One of the great Sumerian cities, in southern Babylonia, about 40 miles/64km north-west of Ur. It is mentioned in Genesis in the list of nations.
Genesis 10:10; Ezra 4:9/3

**Eshcol** A valley near Hebron. The name means 'a cluster of grapes'. When Moses sent spies into the Promised Land they brought back samples of the fruit of the country, including a huge bunch of grapes from this valley.
Numbers 13:23–24; 32:9;
Deuteronomy 1:24

**Eshtaol** A place about 10 miles/16 km west of Jerusalem, on the borders of the land belonging to the tribe of Dan. This was the home district of Samson. Here he grew up, and the Spirit of God first moved him to go out against the Philistines in the lowlands to the west. In spite of Samson's exploits, the Danites never occupied their inheritance.

Joshua 15:33; 19:41; Judges 13:24–25; 16:31; 18/6; B5

**Ethiopia** This is Sudan, not modern Ethiopia, and is called Cush in many translations of the Old Testament. See *Cush* in Part 1: *Environment of the Bible.*

**Euphrates** In the Old Testament this great river is often referred to simply as 'the river'. It is 1,200 miles/1,931km long. It rises in eastern Turkey and flows southeast to the Persian Gulf. Its course through the Babylonian plains has moved west, leaving many of the ancient cities which once stood on its banks now 3–4 miles/5–6km to the east. The route to Syria followed the Euphrates north to Carchemish, then turned south towards Damascus, Israel and Egypt. The Euphrates is mentioned as one of the four rivers of Eden. (See the picture on page 267.)
Genesis 2:14; 15:18, etc.; Revelation 9:14; 16:12/3

**Ezion-geber** See *Elath.*

**Fair Havens** A small port on the south coast of Crete. Paul's ship called in at Fair Havens on the voyage to Rome. Here Paul conferred with the centurion Julius and the owner and captain of the ship, who wanted to reach a more attractive harbour in which to spend the winter. In spite of Paul's advice they put out to sea, and were caught in the violent wind which drove them to shipwreck on Malta.
Acts 27:8–12/15

**Gad** The land belonging to the tribe of Gad. Part of the former Amorite kingdom, east of the River Jordan (south Gilead).
Joshua 13: 8–13/5

**Galatia** A Roman province in central Asia Minor. Its capital was Ancyra (now Ankara, the capital of modern Turkey). Several cities visited by Paul – Pisidian Antioch, Iconium, Lystra and perhaps Derbe – were in the southern part of Galatia, and Paul's letter to the Galatians was probably addressed to them. Galatia was also one of the areas to which 1 Peter was sent.
Acts 16:6; 18:23; Galatians 1:1; 1 Peter 1:1/13

**Galilee** The name of an area and large lake in northern Israel. The home area of Jesus and a number of his disciples. When his public work began, Jesus spent much of his time here.

Galilee is mentioned occasionally in the Old Testament. It was surrounded on three sides by other nations and strongly influenced by them. Most of Galilee is hilly, but the land falls steeply to 600ft/184m below sea level around the lake.

At the time of Jesus several major roads of the Roman Empire crossed Galilee. Farming, trade and the lakeside fisheries were the main industries. Many of the towns and villages mentioned in the Gospels were in Galilee, including Nazareth (where Jesus grew up), Capernaum, Cana and Bethsaida. The lake, which is liable to sudden fierce storms as the wind funnels through the hills that ring it round, is also a focal point in the Gospel stories.
1 Kings 9:11; 2 Kings 15:29; Isaiah 9:1; Luke 4:14; 5:1 and following; 8:22–26; John 21, etc.; Acts 9:31/14; B3

**Gath** One of five Philistine strongholds in Old Testament times. When the Philistines captured the Covenant Box (ark) it was taken to Gath, but plague followed. Goliath came from Gath, the home of other 'giants', too. Later, when David was on the run from King Saul, he escaped to Gath. Soldiers from Gath helped him when his son Absalom led a rebellion against him. The city was subject to the kingdom of Judah for some time and eventually fell to the Assyrians in the eighth century BC. The site is still not certain.
Joshua 11:22; 1 Samuel 5; 17:4; 21:10 – 22:1; 27; 2 Samuel 15:18; 2 Kings 12:17; 2 Chronicles 11:8; 26:6

**Gath-hepher** A place in Galilee on the borders of the lands belonging to the tribes of Zebulun and Naphtali. It was the birth-place of the prophet Jonah. It lay close to the later town of Nazareth.
Joshua 19:13; 2 Kings 14:25 /6; B2

**Gaza** One of five Philistine strongholds in Old Testament times, on the coastal plain. Joshua conquered and then lost the city. The town features in the story of Samson. He was put in prison here, and finally died when he brought about the collapse of a great building. Gaza suffered with the other Philistine cities when they captured the Covenant Box (ark).

The town was an important one on the trade route to Egypt. It was conquered by King Hezekiah of Judah, and later by the Assyrian armies and the Egyptian pharaoh.

In the New Testament, Philip was on the road from Jerusalem to Gaza when he met the Ethiopian official and told him the Good News about Jesus.
Joshua 10:41; Judges 16; 1 Samuel 6:17; 2 Kings 18:8; Jeremiah 47; Acts 8:26/6; A6

**Geba** Modern Jeba', opposite Michmash, 6 miles/10km north of Jerusalem. A city belonging to the tribe of Benjamin. Saul's army camped here in front of his capital at Gibeah when the Philistines held Michmash. Later Geba became the northern limit of the southern kingdom of Judah, and was fortified by King Asa. Like Michmash, it was on the route of the Assyrian approach to Jerusalem, and was resettled after the exile.
Joshua 18:24; 21:17; 1 Samuel 13:16; 1 Kings 15:22; 2 Kings 23:8; 1 Chronicles 6:60; Isaiah 10:29; Ezra 2:26; Nehemiah 7:30; Zechariah 14:10/6; B5

**Gebal** A very ancient Phoenician city, often known by its Greek name Byblos. It was on the coast of modern Lebanon, north of Berytus (Beirut). 'There is still much land to be taken,' God told Joshua in his old age. Gebal was one of the areas included on the list. Later, workmen from Gebal helped to prepare the timber and stone for building Solomon's temple. Ezekiel prophesied against Tyre and other Phoenician towns, including Gebal.
Joshua 13:5; 1 Kings 5:18; Psalm 83:9; Ezekiel 27:9/7

**Gennesaret** A place on the western shore of Lake Galilee. The name is also used of the lake itself. See also *Galilee, Chinnereth.*
Mark 6:53; Luke 5:1

**Gerar** A place in the Negev, between Beersheba and Gaza, where both Abraham and Isaac stayed. For safety, Abraham said that his wife Sarah was his sister. Abimelech, king of Gerar, wanted to take Sarah as his wife. But God prevented this.
Genesis 20:26/6; A6

**Gerizim** The mountain of God's blessing, in Samaria, opposite Mt Ebal (see *Ebal*). Gerizim later became the Samaritans' sacred mountain, the place where they built their temple. It was the mountain which the woman of Samaria mentioned as the place where her ancestors worshipped. The site of the ancient Samaritan temple has recently been found on a spur of Mt Gerizim.
Deuteronomy 11:29; 27;
Joshua 8:33; John 4:20/6; B4

**Geshur** A region and town in southern Syria. King David married the king of Geshur's daughter. Their son, Absalom, fled to Geshur after he had killed his half-brother Amnon in revenge for the rape of his sister Tamar.
Joshua 12:5; 2 Samuel 3:3;
13:38, etc./7

**Gethsemane** ('olive press'). A garden across the Kidron Valley from Jerusalem, close to the Mount of Olives. Jesus and his disciples often went there. So Judas knew where to take the soldiers on the night of the arrest.
Matthew 26:36–56; Mark 14:32–51; Luke 22:39; John 18:1–12

**Gezer** One of the Canaanite towns Joshua campaigned against. It was in the low hills, on the road from Joppa (on the coast) to Jerusalem. Gezer belonged to Egypt for a while until one of the pharaohs gave it to his daughter, King Solomon's wife. Solomon fortified the town, with Hazor and Megiddo. It is the place where archaeologists discovered the 'Gezer calendar' (see Part 8: *Work and Society in the Bible*, under *Farming*).
Joshua 10:33, etc.; 1 Kings 9:15–17/6; B5

**Gibeah** A hill-top town 3 miles/4km north of Jerusalem, which became famous as the home and capital city of King Saul. The place had been tragically destroyed as a result of a crime committed by its people during the time of the Judges. The site is at Tell el-Ful, overlooking the suburbs of Jerusalem.
Judges 19:12 – 20:48;
1 Samuel 10:26, etc.; Isaiah 10:29/6; B5

**Gibeon** A town about 6 miles/10 km north-west of Jerusalem. After the fall of Jericho and Ai the Gibeonites tricked Joshua into a peace treaty. Saul later broke this. David's men fought the supporters of Saul's son Ishbosheth at the pool of Gibeon, to decide which should be king. The tent of worship (tabernacle) was kept at Gibeon, and King Solomon worshipped there. The people of Gibeon helped Nehemiah to rebuild the walls of Jerusalem.
Archaeologists have discovered a huge pit at Gibeon, with a stairway leading down to water. Inside it there were handles of a great many storage jars, each one inscribed with the name 'Gibeon' and the owner's name. The town seems to have been an important centre for wine-making in the seventh century BC.
Joshua 9; 2 Samuel 2:12–29; 20:8; 21; 1 Kings 3:4; 1 Chronicles 21:29; Nehemiah 3:7/6; B5

**Gihon** The name of one of the four great rivers which flowed out of the Garden of Eden.
Gihon was also the name of a spring at the foot of the hill on which the first city of Jerusalem stood. It was then the main source of water for the city. Solomon was anointed king at this spring by the command of his father David, to forestall the attempt of his rival Adonijah to seize the throne. The Gihon spring water was vitally important to the safety of the city and, later, King Hezekiah cut a tunnel to bring the water right through the hill and inside the walls. This tunnel still exists. The water comes out at the Pool of Siloam (see *Siloam*).
Genesis 2:13; 1 Kings 1;
2 Chronicles 32:30; 33:14

**Gilboa** A mountain and range in the north of Palestine, overlooking the deep Valley of Jezreel which runs down to the River Jordan. King Saul and his army took their last stand against the Philistines on Mt Gilboa. Saul, Jonathan and his other two sons

Trawlers fishing on Lake Galilee.

were all killed there.
1 Samuel 28:4; 31:1, 8; 2 Samuel 1; 21:12; 1 Chronicles 10:1, 8 /6; B3

**Gilead** A large area east of the River Jordan, extending north from the Dead Sea. The tribes of Reuben, Gad and Manasseh each occupied part of Gilead. The region was good grazing-land, famous for its flocks and herds. It was also famous for a gum or spice known as the 'balm' of Gilead. This was used to heal wounds, and also as a cosmetic. Jair, Jephthah and the prophet Elijah

all came from Gilead.
Genesis 37:25; Joshua 17:1;
Judges 10:3; 11; 1 Kings 17:1;
Song of Solomon 4:1/6; C3

**Gilgal** A place between Jericho and the River Jordan. The Israelites camped at Gilgal after crossing the river, and set up stones to mark the event. From Gilgal they set out to conquer Canaan. It became the site of an important shrine, and was on Samuel's circuit as a Judge. Gilgal is mentioned in the stories of Elijah and also of Elisha, who dealt with a pot of 'poisoned' stew there. The prophets Hosea and Amos condemned the worship at Gilgal as empty ritual.
Joshua 4:20; Judges 3:19;
1 Samuel 7:16; 10:8, etc.;
2 Samuel 19:15; 2 Kings 2:1;
4:38–41; Hosea 4:15;
Amos 4:4/6; C5

**Gomorrah** One of five cities probably now beneath the southern end of the Dead Sea. Gomorrah was violently destroyed with Sodom for deliberate, persistent and vicious sin. Throughout the Bible, Sodom and Gomorrah are used as examples to warn God's people of his judgement. Jesus says that any town which refuses to hear his messengers is in a worse situation than Sodom and Gomorrah.
Genesis 14; 19; Isaiah 1:9–10;
(Ezekiel 16:48–50); Matthew 10:15

**Goshen** A fertile area of the eastern Nile Delta in Egypt. When Jacob and his family went to join Joseph, they settled in Goshen. It was a good place for their flocks and herds, and it was close to Pharaoh's court. In the time just before the exodus, the Israelites in Goshen escaped the plagues suffered by the rest of Egypt.
Genesis 45:10; Exodus 8:22, etc./4

**Gozan** Israelites from Samaria were taken captive to Gozan by the Assyrians. The town is modern Tell Halaf on the River Khabur in north-east Syria.
2 Kings 17:6; 19:12/9

**Great Sea** The Bible often uses this name for the Mediterranean Sea.

**Greece** The conquests of Alexander the Great brought Israel (and the rest of the eastern Mediterranean lands) under Greek control. The influence of Greek civilization, culture and thought was strong in the last centuries before Christ and in New Testament times. See *The Greeks* in Part 1: *Environment of the Bible*; also Part 5: *Religion and Worship in the Bible,* under *Greek and Roman Religion,* and *Between the Testaments.*
Daniel 11; John 12:20; Acts 6; 17; 18/11

**Habor** The River Khabur in north-east Syria. A tributary of the River Euphrates. The town of Gozan was on the Habor River.
2 Kings 17:6/9

**Hamath** Modern Hama, on the River Orontes in Syria. In Old Testament times Hamath was an important town, capital of a small kingdom, and on a main trade-route from Asia Minor (Turkey) south to Israel and Egypt. Hamath Pass, some distance to the south, was the 'ideal' northern limit of Israel. In the reigns of David and Solomon, Israel had a peace treaty with King Toi of Hamath. The town fell to the Assyrians and many of its people were moved into Israel. First Pharaoh Neco (before the Battle of Carchemish) and then King Nebuchadnezzar of Babylon made it their headquarters for a time.
Joshua 13:5; 2 Samuel 8:9–11; 1 Kings 8:65; 2 Chronicles 8:4; 2 Kings 17:24; 18:34, etc./7·

**Harran** A town in what is now south-east Turkey, on the River Balikh, a tributary of the River Euphrates. This was the place where Abraham's father, Terah,

Beehive houses at Harran in Syria, the town where Abraham stayed on his way from Ur, nearly 4,000 years ago.

settled after leaving Ur, and where Jacob worked for Laban. Harran was on the main road linking Nineveh with Aleppo in Syria, and on south to the port of Tyre. It was fortified by the Assyrians as a provincial capital. For three years after the fall of Nineveh it was Assyria's capital city. Then in 609 BC it fell to the Babylonians.
Genesis 11:31; 12:4–5; 29:4, etc.; 2 Kings 19:12; Ezekiel 27:33/4

**Harod** The spring where Gideon chose his fighting-force by watching how the men drank from the stream. The 300 who showed their alertness by stooping and lapping the water were chosen. The place was in northern Palestine, probably by a stream which flows down the Valley of Jezreel.
Judges 7:1–8

**Hazor** A Canaanite city in the north of Israel. King Jabin of Hazor organized an alliance against Joshua. But he was defeated, and the city was burned. Another king of Hazor was defeated by Deborah and Barak. King Solomon rebuilt and fortified Hazor, with Megiddo and Gezer. In the eighth century BC the Assyrians destroyed the city.

Archaeologists have uncovered an upper and a lower city, which at its greatest may have housed as many as 40,000 people. The lower part was destroyed in the thirteenth century BC (about the time of Joshua). A city gate and wall from Solomon's time match others of the same design at Megiddo and Gezer. Hazor is mentioned in Egyptian and Babylonian texts, and in the Amarna Letters, as well as in the Bible itself. See Part 2: *Archaeology and the Bible.*
Joshua 11; Judges 4; 1 Kings 9:15; 2 Kings 15:29/6; C2

**Hebron** A town high in the Judean hills (3,040ft/935m above sea level). The old name for Hebron was Kiriath-arba. Abraham and his family often camped near Hebron. He bought the cave of Machpelah from the Hittites at Hebron (see *Machpelah*). Moses' twelve spies came to Hebron, and it was later given to Caleb. Hebron was a city of refuge, and one of the Levites' towns. It was David's capital before he captured Jerusalem. Absalom staged his rebellion from Hebron. Much later, after the exile, Jews returned to live there.
Genesis 13:18; 23; 35:27; 37:14; Numbers 13:22; Joshua 14:6–15; 2 Samuel 2:1–4; 15:9–10; Nehemiah 11:25/6; B6

**Heliopolis** See *On.*

**Hermon** A mountain on the Lebanon/Syria border. It is over 9,000ft/2,750m high. It is also called Sirion in the Bible. It is topped with snow almost all the year round. The melting snow and ice form a major source of the River Jordan. Mt Hermon is close to Caesarea Philippi and may be the 'high mountain' where Jesus' disciples saw him in his glory.
Joshua 12:1, etc.; Psalm 42:6;

133:3; Matthew 17:1, etc./*14; C1*

**Heshbon** A town east of the River Jordan which belonged first to Moab, then to the Amorites, and then to the Israelite tribes of Reuben and Gad. It was prosperous for a while at the time of Isaiah and Jeremiah.
Numbers 21:25–30; 32:37; Isaiah 15:4; Jeremiah 48:2/*6; C5*

**Hierapolis** A city in the Roman province of Asia, now in western Turkey. Paul mentions the Christians at Laodicea and Hierapolis in his letter to nearby Colossae. Over the centuries the hot-water springs at Hierapolis (modern Pamukkale), have 'petrified' to form amazing waterfalls of stone.
Colossians 4:13/*15*

Mt Hermon, whose snows feed the River Jordan; the view from Dan in the north of Israel.

**Hinnom** The name of a valley on the south side of Jerusalem, forming the boundary between the tribes of Judah and Benjamin. Here the kings Ahaz and Manasseh set up a shrine for the god Molech, and children were offered to him in sacrifice. It was destroyed by Josiah. Jeremiah denounced the evil of this place. Later, rubbish from the city was burned in the Valley of Hinnom. So it became a picture of hell. The word 'Gehenna', meaning 'Valley of Hinnom', became a word for 'hell'.
Joshua 15:8; 18:16; 2 Kings 23:10; 2 Chronicles 28:3; 33:6; Jeremiah 7:31; 19:2; 32:35/*12*

**Horeb** Another name for Mt Sinai.

**Hormah** The exact site of this town in southern Canaan is not certain. Because of their disobedience, the Israelites were defeated by the Canaanites at Hormah. Later it was conquered and given to the tribe of Judah.
Numbers 14:39–45; 21:3; Joshua 15:30

**Ibleam** A Canaanite town in the north of Israel, about 10 miles/14km south-east of Megiddo. Here Jehu killed King Ahaziah of Judah.
Joshua 17:11–12; 2 Kings 9:27; 15:10/*6; B3*

**Iconium** Present-day Konya in south-central Turkey. Paul preached at Iconium, then a town in the Roman province of Galatia, on his first missionary journey. He met with violent opposition.
Acts 13:51; 14:1–6, 19–22; 2 Timothy 3:11/*15*

**Idumaea** The Greek name for the Old Testament Edom. By New Testament times many Idumaeans had settled west of the Jordan, in the dry country in the south of Palestine. This district was then called Idumaea. King Herod was an Idumaean. People came even from this area in the far south to see Jesus in Galilee.
Mark 3:8/*14; A7*

**Illyricum** The Roman name of a land stretching along the eastern shore of the Adriatic Sea. It covered much the same area as modern Yugoslavia. The southern part was also called Dalmatia (see *Dalmatia*). When Paul wrote to the Romans, he said he had preached the gospel from Jerusalem as far west as Illyricum. There is no other mention of Paul's work in this land.
Romans 15:19/*13*

**Israel** The land occupied by the twelve tribes. After King Solomon died and his kingdom was divided, the name Israel referred to the northern part of the land, excluding Judah and Benjamin. See Part 1: *Environment of the Bible, The Geography of the Land of Israel,* and Part 10: *Atlas of the Bible.*

**Issachar** The land belonging to the tribe of Issachar, south of Lake Galilee and west of the River Jordan.
Joshua 19:17–23/*5*

**Ituraea** A name mentioned only in Luke's careful dating of the time when John the Baptist began to preach. Herod Philip was then ruler of Ituraea and Trachonitis. The Ituraeans were probably the descendants of the Old Testament people called Jetur. They were a wild tribal people in the hills west of Damascus, north of the headwaters of the River Jordan. See also *Trachonitis.*
Luke 3:1; compare 1 Chronicles 5:19/*14; C1*

**Jabbok** Now the Zerqa, a river that flows into the Jordan from the east, between the Dead Sea and Lake Galilee. Jacob wrestled with an angel beside the Jabbok. Adam – the place where the Jordan was dammed, allowing the Israelites to cross into the Promised Land – stands at the confluence of the Jabbok and the Jordan. The river is also mentioned in the Bible as a boundary.
Genesis 32:22–30; Numbers 21:24; Deuteronomy 3:16; Judges 11:13/*6; C4*

**Jabesh-gilead** A town on the east of the Jordan. When the wives of the Benjaminites were killed in a civil war at the time of the Judges, the town of Jabesh provided replacements. Saul answered an appeal for help when Jabesh was besieged by the Ammonites. Men from Jabesh later risked their lives to remove his body from Beth-shan.
Judges 21; 1 Samuel 11; 31:11–13/*6; C4*

**Javan** One of the sons of Japheth. Javan is named as the father of a group of peoples, probably including those who lived in Greece and Asia Minor in early times. The name may be connected with the Greek 'Ionia', in western Turkey, and it is used in later parts of the Old Testament for Greece or the Greeks.
Genesis 10:2; 1 Chronicles 1:5; Isaiah 66:19; Ezekiel 27:13

**Jazer** An Amorite town east of the River Jordan. It was captured by the Israelites and given to the tribe of Gad. Jazer was famous for its vines.
Numbers 21:32; Joshua 13:25; 1 Chronicles 26:31; Isaiah 16:8–9/*6; C4*

**Jebus** An early name for Jerusalem.

**Jericho** A town west of the River Jordan, 820ft/250m below sea level, about 5 miles/8km from the northern end of the Dead Sea. Jericho's fresh-water spring makes it an oasis in the surrounding desert – the 'city of palm trees'. The town guarded the fords of the Jordan, across which Joshua sent his spies. It was well fortified, and the first main obstacle facing the invading Israelites. Joshua gained his first victory in the land when Jericho fell.

At the time of the Judges Ehud killed King Eglon of Moab at Jericho. At the time of Elijah and Elisha it was the home of a large group of prophets. After the return from exile, men from Jericho helped rebuild the walls of Jerusalem.

In the New Testament Jesus gave Bartimaeus his sight, and Zacchaeus became a changed man, at Jericho. The story of the Good Samaritan is set on the road from Jerusalem to Jericho.

Jericho has a very long history covering thousands of years. The first town was built here some time before 6000 BC. At the time of Abraham, Isaac and Jacob, life in Jericho was a civilized affair. In tombs from about 1600 BC, fine pottery, wooden furniture, basket-work, and boxes with inlaid decoration have been found. Some time after this Jericho was destroyed, but a small settlement remained. See Part 2: *Archaeology and the Bible* and Part 4: *Key Teaching and Events of the Bible,* under *The Conquest.*
Joshua 2; 6; Judges 12:13;
2 Kings 2; Nehemiah 3:2;
Mark 10:46; Luke 19:1–10;
10:30/6; C5

**Jerusalem** Capital of Israel's early kings, later of the southern kingdom of Judah, and one of the world's most famous cities. Jerusalem stands high (2,500ft/ 770m) in the Judean hills with no access by sea or river. The ground drops steeply away on all sides except the north. To the east, between Jerusalem (with its temple) and the Mount of Olives, is the Kidron Valley. The Valley of Hinnom curves around the city to the south and west. A third, central valley cuts right into the city, dividing the temple area and city of David from the 'upper', western section.

Jerusalem is probably the 'Salem' of which Melchizedek was king in Abraham's day. It was certainly in existence by 1800 BC. It was a Jebusite stronghold (called Jebus) when King David captured it and made it his capital. He bought the temple site and brought the Covenant Box (ark) to Jerusalem. Solomon built the

The oasis town of Jericho. The small white hut in the middle distance marks the mound (tell) of the ancient town which flourished many centuries before Joshua's day.

temple for God, and from that time on Jerusalem has been the 'holy city' – for the Jews, and later for Christians and Muslims, too. Solomon added fine palaces and public buildings. Jerusalem was a political and religious centre, to which the people came for the great annual festivals.

The city declined to some extent after Solomon, when the kingdom became divided. In the reign of King Hezekiah (Isaiah's time) it was besieged by the Assyrians. The king had the Siloam tunnel built, to ensure his water supply (see Part 2: *Archaeology and the Bible*). On several occasions powerful neighbouring kings were pacified with treasures from the city and its temple. The Babylonians besieged Jerusalem in 597 BC and in 586 they captured and destroyed both the city and the temple. The people were taken into exile.

In 538 BC they were allowed to return. Under Zerubbabel's leadership the temple was rebuilt. With Nehemiah in charge they rebuilt the city walls. In 198 BC, as part of the Greek Empire, Jerusalem came under the control of the Syrian Seleucid kings. One of these, Antiochus IV Epiphanes plundered and desecrated the temple. Judas Maccabaeus led a Jewish revolt and the temple was rededicated (164 BC).

For a time Jerusalem was free. Then, in the middle of the first century BC, the Romans took control. Herod the Great, made king by the Romans, repaired Jerusalem and undertook new building work, including a magnificent new temple.

It was to this temple that Jesus' mother brought him as a baby. His parents brought him again when he was twelve, to attend the annual Passover Festival. When he grew up, Jesus regularly visited Jerusalem – for many of the religious festivals, and to teach and heal. His arrest, trial, crucifixion and resurrection all took place in Jerusalem.

Jesus' followers were still in the city several weeks later, on the Day of Pentecost, when the Holy Spirit made new men of them. So the Christian church began life in Jerusalem – and from there, spread out far and wide. The Christians at Jerusalem played a leading role in the early years. The Council that met to consider the position of non-Jewish Christians was held at Jerusalem.

In AD 66 the Jews rose in revolt against the Romans. In AD 70 the Romans regained Jerusalem. They destroyed its defences – and the temple. Not until the fourth century – the reign of Constantine – were Jews again allowed to live in Jerusalem. The city became Christian, and many churches were built.

In 637 the Muslims came – and Jerusalem remained under their control for most of the time until 1948, when the modern state of Israel came into being. Jerusalem was then divided between the Jews and the Arabs – Israel and Jordan. In 1967 the Jews won control of the whole city.

See the special feature on Jerusalem in Part 10: *Atlas of the Bible.* See also Part 2: *Archaeology and the Bible.*
Genesis 14:18; Joshua 15:63; 2 Samuel 5; 1 Kings 6; Psalms 48; 122; 125; 1 Kings 14:25–26; 2 Kings 12:18; 18:13 – 19:36; 20:20; 25; Ezra 5; Nehemiah 3 – 6; Luke 2; 19:28 – 24:49, etc.; John 2:23 – 3:21; 5; 7:10 – 10:42, etc.; Acts 2; 15/*6; B5*

**Jezreel** A town in the north of Israel and the plain in which it stood, close to Mt Gilboa. Saul camped at the spring in the Valley of Jezreel before the Battle of Gilboa. King Ahab of Israel had a palace at Jezreel. It was here that the sad story of Naboth's vineyard took place. King Joram of Israel went to Jezreel to recover from his wounds. Queen Jezebel was thrown down from the palace window and died here.
1 Samuel 29:1; 1 Kings 18:45–46; 21; 2 Kings 8:29; 9:30–37/*6; B3*

A street in the old city of Jerusalem.

**Joppa** The only natural harbour on the coast of Israel south of the Bay of Acre (Haifa): modern Jaffa, close to Tel Aviv. Joppa was the port for Jerusalem, 35 miles/56km away. The town has a long history and was mentioned about 1400 BC in the Egyptian Amarna Letters. Jonah set sail for Tarshish (Spain) from Joppa. Dorcas (Tabitha), the woman Peter restored to life, came from Joppa. Peter was there when he had his dream about the 'clean' and 'unclean' animals. He went from Joppa to the house of the Roman officer, Cornelius, and saw God at work amongst non-Jews.
2 Chronicles 2:16; Jonah 1:3; Acts 9:36–43; 10/*6; A4*

**Jordan** The main river of Israel, constantly referred to in the Bible. The Jordan flows from Mt Hermon in the far north, through Lake Huleh, and Lake Galilee to the Dead Sea. It is 75 miles/120km from Lake Huleh to the Dead Sea, but the river winds about so much that it is more than twice that length.

The name 'Jordan' means 'the descender'. It flows through the deepest rift valley on earth. Lake Huleh is 230ft/71m above sea level. Lake Galilee is nearly 700ft/215m *below* sea level, and the north end of the Dead Sea 1,290ft/397m below.

The northern part of the Jordan Valley is fertile; the southern end, approaching the Dead Sea, is desert, but dense jungle grows on the banks. The main tributaries of the Jordan are the Yarmuk and Jabbok rivers, both of which join it from the east. Many smaller tributaries dry up completely through the summer.

Joshua led the people of Israel across the Jordan from the east into the Promised Land near to Jericho. At the time of Absalom's rebellion, David escaped across the Jordan. Elijah and Elisha crossed the Jordan just before Elijah was taken up to heaven. Elisha told the Syrian general Naaman to wash himself in the Jordan and he would be healed. John the Baptist baptized people – including Jesus – in the Jordan.
Joshua 3; 2 Samuel 17:20-22; 2 Kings 2:6–8, 13–14; 5; Jeremiah 12:5; 49:19; Mark 1:5, 9, etc./*6*

**Judah** The Judean hills south of Jerusalem and the desert bordering the Dead Sea. The land belonging to the tribe of Judah. Later the name of the southern kingdom, with Jerusalem as its capital.
Joshua 15; 1 Kings 12:21, 23, etc./*6; B6*

**Judea** The Greek and Roman name for Judah. Usually it refers to the southern part of the country, with Jerusalem as capital. But it is sometimes used as a name for the whole land, including Galilee and Samaria. The 'wilderness of Judea' is the desert west of the Dead Sea.
Luke 3:1; 4:44 ('the whole country' in *Good News Bible*), etc. /*14; B5*

**Kadesh-barnea** An oasis and settlement in the desert south of Beersheba. It is mentioned in the campaign of Chedorlaomer and his allies at the time of Abraham . It was near Kadesh that Hagar saw an angel. After the escape from Egypt, most of Israel's years of desert wandering were spent in the area around Kadesh. Miriam died there, and Moses brought water out of the rock. From Kadesh he sent spies into Canaan. It is later mentioned as a point on the southern boundary of Israel.
Genesis 14:7; 16:14; Numbers 20; 13; 33:36; Deuteronomy 1:19–25, 46; Joshua 10:41; 15:23 (Kedesh) /*5*

The springs which feed the River Jordan in the north of Israel make it a sizeable river almost from its source.

**Kedesh** A Canaanite town in Galilee conquered by Joshua and given to the tribe of Naphtali. It was the home of Barak. Kedesh was one of the first towns to fall to the Assyrians when Tiglath-

pileser III invaded Israel from the north (734-732 BC).
Joshua 12:22; 19:37; Judges 4; 2 Kings 15:29/*6; C1*

**Keilah** A town about 8 miles/11km north-west of Hebron. David saved it from a Philistine attack and stayed there, escaping from Saul.
Joshua 15:44; 1 Samuel 23; Nehemiah 3:17–18/*6; B5*

**Kidron** The valley which separates Jerusalem and the temple from the Mount of Olives, on the east. For most of the year the valley is dry. The Gihon Spring, whose water King Hezekiah brought inside the city walls through the Siloam tunnel, is on the west side of the Kidron Valley.

David crossed the Kidron when he left Jerusalem at the time of Absalom's rebellion. Asa, Hezekiah and Josiah, kings who reformed the nation's worship, destroyed idols in the Kidron Valley. Jesus and his disciples crossed it many times on their way to the Garden of Gethsemane.
2 Samuel 15:23; 1 Kings 15:13; 2 Chronicles 29:16; 2 Kings 23:4; John 18:1/*12*

**King's Highway** The road by which Moses promised to travel peacefully through the land of Edom and the land of Sihon, king of Heshbon. Both refused his request, and so the Israelites were forced to avoid Edom and to fight and defeat Sihon. The King's Highway was probably the main route north to south along the heights east of the Jordan, between Damascus and the Gulf of Aqaba.
Numbers 20:17; 21:22; Deuteronomy 2:27/*5*

**Kir, Kir-hareseth** The name of an unknown place where the Syrians were exiled.

An important fortified town in Moab.
2 Kings 16:9; Amos 1:5; 2 Kings 3; Isaiah 16:7–12/*6; C7*

**Kiriathaim** A town east of the Dead Sea given to the tribe of Reuben. It was later taken by the Moabites.
Joshua 13:19; Jeremiah 48:1–25; Ezekiel 25:9/*6; C6*

Laodicea, in the beautiful Lycus Valley of Turkey. The town was prosperous in New Testament times. One of the letters in the Book of Revelation was written to the church at Laodicea.

**Kiriath-arba** An earlier name for Hebron.

**Kiriath-jearim** A hill-town a few miles east of Jerusalem. It was one of the towns of the Gibeonites, who tricked Joshua into a peace treaty. The Covenant Box (ark) was kept at Kiriath-jearim for twenty years before King David took it to Jerusalem.
Joshua 9; 1 Samuel 6:20 – 7:2; Jeremiah 26:20; Nehemiah 7:29/*6; B5*

**Kishon** A small stream which flows across the plain of Megiddo (Esdraelon) and into the Mediterranean Sea just north of Mt Carmel. In the story of Barak heavy rain raised the water level so high that the surrounding ground turned to mud and bogged down Sisera's chariots, giving Israel victory. The prophet Elijah killed the prophets of Baal by the River Kishon after the contest on Mt Carmel.
Judges 4; 5:21; 1 Kings 18:40/*6; B2*

**Kittim** One of the sons of Javan in the Genesis 'table of the nations', and so the name of Cyprus and of its early city of Kition (modern Larnaca). See *Cypriotes* in Part 1: *Environment of the Bible.*
Genesis 10:4; 1 Chronicles 1:7; Numbers 24:24; Isaiah 23:1, 12; Jeremiah 2:10; Ezekiel 27:6

**Kue/Coa** A region from which Solomon obtained horses. It was

in the eastern part of Cilicia, in the south of modern Turkey.

**Lachish** An important fortified town in the low hills about 30 miles/48km south-west of Jerusalem. Lachish has a long history. It was a military stronghold before the sixteenth century BC.

The king of Lachish joined with four other Amorite kings to fight Joshua. But Joshua won. He attacked and captured Lachish and put everyone there to death.

Solomon's son, King Rehoboam, rebuilt Lachish as a defence against the Philistines and Egyptians.

The town had an outer and inner wall, 19ft/6m thick. These walls were strengthened with towers. So too was the gateway. A well 144ft/44m deep ensured a good supply of water. Lachish had a palace and store-rooms approached by a street lined with shops.

King Amaziah of Judah fled to Lachish for safety. But his enemies followed and killed him there.

When the Assyrian King Sennacherib attacked Judah he besieged Lachish, cutting Jerusalem off from possible help from Egypt. He sent envoys from Lachish to demand Jerusalem's surrender. Lachish fell, and Sennacherib had the siege pictured on the walls of his palace at Nineveh. Archaeologists have also discovered at Lachish a mass grave from this time, holding 1,500 bodies.

A grove of ancient cedars on the mountain slopes of Lebanon. In Old Testament times the whole area was forested with these beautiful and valuable trees.

The Babylonian army attacked Lachish at the time of the final siege of Jerusalem (589–586 BC). The 'Lachish Letters', written by an army officer to his superior, belong to this period (see Part 2: *Archaeology and the Bible*). Lachish fell and the Babylonians burnt it. After the exile it was resettled, but was never again an important place.
Joshua 10; 2 Chronicles 11:5–12; 2 Kings 14:19; 18:14–21; Isaiah 36 – 37; Jeremiah 34:7; Nehemiah 11:30/*6; A6*

**Laodicea** A town in the Lycus Valley of present-day western Turkey (the Roman province of Asia in New Testament times). Laodicea stood at the junction of two important main roads. It grew prosperous from trade and banking. The region produced clothes made of glossy black wool, and also medicines. Water for the town was piped from hot springs some distance away. A number of these points are reflected in the letter to the church at Laodicea in the Book of Revelation. Paul's letter to the Colossians was intended for Laodicea, too, although he had not been there. The Christian group there may have been started during the time when Paul was staying at Ephesus.
Colossians 2:1; 4:13–16; Revelation 1:11; 3:14–22/*15*

**Lebanon** The modern country of that name and its mountain range. Lebanon in the Old Testament was famous for its forests, especially its great cedar-trees. The Bible refers also to the snows of Lebanon, and to the country's fertility. All kinds of fruit grow on the coastal plain and lower hill slopes: olives, grapes, apples, figs, apricots, dates and all kinds of green vegetables.

The great Phoenician (Canaanite) ports of Tyre, Sidon and Byblos were all on the coast of Lebanon and grew rich exporting its products. See Part 1: *Environment of the Bible,* under *Canaanites* and *Phoenicians.* King Solomon sent to the king of Tyre for cedar and other wood from Lebanon to build the temple and royal palace at Jerusalem.
1 Kings 5:1–11; Hosea 6:5–7; Ezra 3:7; Psalm 72:16; Isaiah 2:13; 14:8; Ezekiel 31, etc.

**Libnah** A fortified lowland town not far from Lachish, taken by Joshua. In the reign of King Jehoram of Judah Libnah rebelled. The town survived a siege by the Assyrian King Sennacherib when plague hit his army.
Joshua 10:29–30; 2 Kings 8:22; 19:8, 35/*6; A5*

**Lo-debar** A place in Gilead, east of the River Jordan. Mephibosheth, Jonathan's son, lived

there in exile until David brought him to his court.
2 Samuel 9; 17:27/*6; C3*

**Lud** Lud, a son of Shem, gave his name to a people known later as the Lydians. They lived in the west of Asia Minor (Turkey) around Sardis. See *Lydians* in Part 1: *Environment of the Bible*.

**Luz** The older name of Bethel.

**Lycia** A small, mountainous land in the south-west of Asia Minor (Turkey). The ports of Patara and Myra, at which Paul landed, were in Lycia.
Acts 27:5/*13*

**Lydda** A town about 10 miles/16km inland from Joppa. Peter healed a lame man, Aeneas, when visiting the first Christians here. The place is now again called by its Old Testament name, Lod.
Acts 9:32-35, 38/*14; B5*

**Lystra** A remote town in the Roman province of Galatia (not far from Konya in modern Turkey). Paul and Barnabas went on to Lystra after rough treatment at Iconium, on the first missionary journey. Paul healed a cripple at Lystra, and the people believed him to be Hermes (messenger of the Greek gods) and Barnabas to be Zeus himself. But Jews from Iconium stirred up trouble, and Paul was stoned and left for dead. Some of the people became Christians, and Paul returned to visit them on his second journey. Lystra (or possibly Derbe) was Timothy's home town.
Acts 14:6–20; 16:1–5/*15*

**Maacah** A small Aramaean state to the south-east of Mt Hermon. It is mentioned in David's campaigns and one of his warriors came from here.
Joshua 12:5; 2 Samuel 10; 23:34/*6; C1*

**Macedonia** A region of Greece stretching north and west from Thessalonica. The Roman province of Macedonia included Philippi and Beroea as well as Thessalonica.

Paul crossed the Aegean Sea from Troas after seeing a vision of a Macedonian man asking him to come over and help them. It was

the first stage in bringing the Good News of Jesus to Europe. Three of Paul's letters (Philippians, 1 and 2 Thessalonians) are addressed to Macedonian Christians. They gave generously to his relief fund for Christians in Judea. And several of them became his regular helpers.
Acts 16:8 – 17:15; 20:1–6; 2 Corinthians 8:1–5; 9:1–5, etc. /*13*

**Machpelah** When Sarah died at Hebron, Abraham still owned no land. So he bought a plot of land with the cave of Machpelah from Ephron the Hittite. Abraham himself was later buried here, and afterwards Isaac and Rebekah, and then Jacob.

Much later, Herod the Great built a shrine round the place believed to contain the cave and the tombs, and this can still be seen.
Genesis 23; 25:9; 49:30; 50:13

**Mahanaim** A place in Gilead, east of the River Jordan and near the River Jabbok. Jacob saw God's angels at Mahanaim, before the reunion with his brother Esau. For a short time it was the capital of Saul's son Ishbosheth (Ishbaal). It was King David's headquarters during Absalom's rebellion. One of Solomon's district officers was based at Mahanaim.
Genesis 32:2; 2 Samuel 2:8–10; 17:24–29; 1 Kings 4:14/*6; C4*

**Makkedah** Joshua captured this Canaanite town in the south. In a nearby cave he found the five Amorite kings who had fought against him and killed them. The town was given to the tribe of Judah.
Joshua 10:10, 16; 15:41/*6; B5*

**Malta** The modern name of an island in the central Mediterranean Sea, between Sicily and the north coast of Africa. Its ancient name was Melita, and Paul's ship was wrecked here during his voyage as a prisoner to Rome. All the people on board reached land safely and were received kindly by the natives. They spent the winter on Malta before sailing for Italy.
Acts 28:1–10

**Mamre** A place near Hebron. Abraham, and later Isaac, often camped by the oak-trees at Mamre. It was here that Abraham heard that Lot had been captured.

At Mamre God promised him a son, and he pleaded with God to spare Sodom.
Genesis 13:18; 14:13; 18; 23:17; 35:27/*4*

**Manasseh** The land belonging to the tribe of Manasseh. West Manasseh was the hill-country of Samaria as far west as the Mediterranean Sea. East Manasseh was the land east of central Jordan.
Joshua 13:29–31; 17:7–13/*5*

**Maon** A town in the hills of Judah. Nabal, husband of Abigail, lived here. David stayed here twice when he was an outlaw from King Saul.
Joshua 15:55; 1 Samuel 23:24–25; 25/*6; B6*

**Mareshah** A town in the low hills nearly 20 miles/32 km south-west of Jerusalem. It was fortified by Rehoboam. Later King Asa destroyed a great army from Sudan here. The prophet Micah foretold disaster for Mareshah.
Joshua 15:44; 2 Chronicles 11:8; 14:9–12; 20:37; Micah 1:15/*6; A6*

**Media** North-west Iran. Media came under Assyrian control, but later helped the Babylonians to overthrow the Assyrians. Then Cyrus the Persian brought Media under his control. See *Medes* and Map in Part 1: *Environment of the Bible* and Part 10: *Atlas of the Bible*.

**Megiddo** An important Old Testament city on the edge of the plain of Jezreel, guarding the main pass through the Carmel hills. About 20 miles/32 km from modern Haifa. So many battles took place here that the New Testament (Revelation 16:16) uses the name symbolically for the site of the great last battle: 'Armageddon', 'the hill of Megiddo'.

Joshua defeated the Canaanite king of Megiddo when the Israelites conquered Canaan. It was given to the tribe of Manasseh. They made the Canaanites who lived at Megiddo work for them, but did not drive them out. King Solomon chose Megiddo, with Hazor and Gezer, to be one of his main fortified cities, with stabling for large numbers of horses and chariots. King Ahaziah of Judah died at Megiddo after being wounded by Jehu's men. So too did King Josiah, attempting to stop the advance of Pharaoh Neco of Egypt.

Archaeologists have discovered twenty main levels of settlement on a mound now 70ft/21m high and covering, at the top, an area of more than 10 acres. The earliest settlement goes back to before 3000 BC. Excavation has uncovered, among other things, a Canaanite 'high place'; the city's water supply system; a fortified gateway built to the same pattern as others at Gezer and Hazor; a hoard of carved ivory objects; and a series of stables (probably from King Ahab's time). See Part 2: *Archaeology and the Bible,* also Part 7: *Home and Family Life in the Bible,* under *Town and City Life.*
Joshua 12:21; Judges 1:27–28; 5:19; 1 Kings 9:15; 2 Kings 9:27; 23:29/*6; B3*

**Memphis** The ancient capital of Egypt, on the River Nile not far

south of modern Cairo. The pyramids at Giza are also near to Memphis. The city remained important for many centuries, up to the time of Alexander the Great. Several of the Old Testament prophets refer to Memphis when they condemn Israel's trust in Egypt.
Isaiah 19:13; Jeremiah 2:16; 46:14; Ezekiel 30:13/*3*

**Mesopotamia** The land between the Tigris and Euphrates rivers. Harran and Paddan-aram, where some of Abraham's family settled, are in Mesopotamia. It was the home of Balaam, the prophet who

was sent to curse the Israelites, and the country ruled by Cushan-rishathaim at the time of the Judges.

People from Mesopotamia were in Jerusalem on the Day of Pentecost and heard Peter and the apostles speak to them in their own languages.
Genesis 24:10; Deuteronomy 23:4 and Numbers 22; Judges 3:8, 10; Acts 2:9/*3*

**Michmash** A place about 7 miles/11km north-east of Jerusalem, at a village still called Mukhmas. It was separated from Geba by a deep valley. But an important route, 'the passage of Michmash', crossed an easy part of the valley. The Philistines invaded Israel and camped in force at Michmash, threatening King Saul's capital at Gibeah. Jonathan and his armour-bearer surprised the Philistine garrison

Nazareth in Galilee, the town where Jesus grew up.

by climbing across from Geba at a steep place down the valley, and in the panic which followed Saul defeated the Philistines. Michmash was on the route by which the Assyrians approached Jerusalem from the north. It was reoccupied after the exile.
1 Samuel 13 – 14; Isaiah 10:28; Ezra 2:27; Nehemiah 7:31; 11:31/*6; B5*

**Midian** Part of Arabia, east of the Gulf of Aqaba. See *Midianites* and Map in Part 1: *Environment of the*

*Bible.* When Moses fled for his life from Egypt after killing an Egyptian overseer, he went to Midian. He married a Midianite wife and stayed there until God sent him back to Egypt to help free the Israelites. At the time of the Judges Gideon defeated a huge force of camel-riding invaders from Midian.
Genesis 25:1–6; Exodus 2:15–21; Judges 6/*3*

**Miletus** A sea-port on the west coast of present-day Turkey. Paul stayed at Miletus on his way to Jerusalem at the end of his third missionary journey. To save time, the elders from the church at Ephesus came to meet him there and heard his farewell message. At another time Paul, writing to Timothy, says that he had left his helper Trophimus at Miletus because he was ill.
Acts 20:15–38; 2 Timothy 4:20/*15*

**Mitylene** The most important city and port on the Greek island of Lesbos, off the west coast of Asia Minor (Turkey). Paul stopped there overnight on his last voyage to Jerusalem.
Acts 20:14/*15*

**Mizpah/Mizpeh** The name (meaning 'watchtower') of a number of different places. When Jacob and Laban made a peace agreement they called the place Mizpah. A Mizpah in Gilead (perhaps the same as Ramoth-gilead) features in the story of Jephthah, at the time of the Judges.

The most important Mizpah is a town a few miles north of Jerusalem. The Israelites met together here at the time of Samuel and the Judges. The town was on Samuel's circuit as a Judge. And at Mizpah he presented Saul to the people as their king. Later, King Asa of Judah fortified the town. After Jerusalem fell to the Babylonians the governor, Gedaliah, lived at Mizpah.
Genesis 31:44–49; Judges 10:17; 11; 20:1; 1 Samuel 7:5–16; 10:17; 1 Kings 15:22; 2 Kings 25:23/*6; B5*

**Moab** The country east of the Dead Sea. The land is a

3000ft/900m plateau cut by deep gorges. Moab was the home of Ruth. The country was often at war with Israel, and was denounced again and again by the prophets. See *Moabites* and Map in Part 1: *Environment of the Bible.*
Judges 3:12–30; Ruth 1;
2 Samuel 8:2; 2 Kings 3;
Isaiah 15, etc./*6; C6*

**Plains of Moab** The place east of the River Jordan opposite Jericho where the Israelites gathered before they crossed into Canaan.
Numbers 22:1; 35:1;
Joshua 13:32/*1*

**Moreh** The hill a few miles northwest of Mt Gilboa where the Midianites camped before Gideon's attack.
Judges 7:1/*6; B3*

**Moresheth/Moresheth-gath** The home town of the prophet Micah, probably near Mareshah in the low country south-west of Jerusalem.
Jeremiah 26:18; Micah 1:1, 14

**Moriah** The mountains to which Abraham was told to go for the sacrifice of his son, Isaac. The writer of 2 Chronicles says that the site of Solomon's temple was 'in Jerusalem, on Mount Moriah'. (The Samaritans claimed that the place of Abraham's sacrifice was not Jerusalem, but Mt Gerizim.)
Genesis 22:2; 2 Chronicles 3:1

**Mount of Olives/Olivet** A 2,700ft/830m hill overlooking Jerusalem and its temple area from the east, across the Kidron Valley. In Jesus' day it was planted with olive trees.

King David passed this way when he fled from Jerusalem at the time of Absalom's rebellion. King Solomon built an altar for idols on the Mount of Olives. Later, during the exile, the prophet Ezekiel saw the dazzling light of God's glory leave Jerusalem and move to the Mount of Olives. The prophet Zechariah foresaw God, on the Day of Judgement, standing on the Mount, which would split in two.

When Jesus rode in triumph into Jerusalem he came from the Mount of Olives. Seeing the city from the Mount, he wept over its fate. When he stayed at Bethany

This relief from the palace walls at Nineveh shows two of the Israelite prisoners captured by King Sennacherib's army.

on his visits to Jerusalem he must have walked into the city round the shoulder of the Mount of Olives. The Garden of Gethsemane, where he prayed on the night of his arrest, was on its lower slopes. From the Mount of Olives Jesus was taken up to heaven.
2 Samuel 15:30; 2 Kings 23:13; Ezekiel 11:23; Zechariah 14:4; Luke 19:29, 37, 41–44; 21:37; 22:39; Acts 1:12, etc./*12*

**Myra** A port in Lycia, in the south-west of modern Turkey, where Paul and his party changed ships on his voyage to Rome. Myra was a regular port for the corn-fleet which carried grain to Rome from Egypt.
Acts 27:5/*15*

**Mysia** A land in the north-west of Asia Minor (Turkey), forming part of the Roman province of Asia. Paul came to this district during his second missionary journey, but God prevented him from crossing the border from Asia into Bithynia. He passed through Mysia, travelling west, and came to Troas before it became clear where he should go next.
Acts 16:7–8/*13*

**Nain** A town near Nazareth in Galilee where Jesus restored a widow's son to life.
Luke 7:11/*14; B3*

**Naphtali** Land belonging to the tribe of Naphtali, in Galilee.
Joshua 19:32–39/*5*

**Nazareth** A town in Galilee, the home of Jesus' parents, Mary and Joseph. Jesus grew up in Nazareth but made his base in Capernaum when he began his public work. His teaching in the synagogue at Nazareth made the people so angry that they tried to kill him.

Nazareth was close to a number of important trade-routes, and so in contact with the wider world. There are rock-tombs at Nazareth dating from New Testament times, and similar to the Gospels' description of the grave in which Jesus himself was buried. (Picture page 277.)
Luke 1:26; Matthew 2:22–23; Luke 2:39, 51; Mark 1:9; Matthew 4:13; Luke 4:16–30; John 1:45–46, etc./*14; B2*

**Neapolis** The port for Philippi, in Macedonia (northern Greece). This was the place where Paul first set foot in Europe, in answer to a call for help from Macedonia. He later sailed from here on his last voyage to Jerusalem. The place is modern Kavalla.
Acts 16:11; 20:6/*15*

**Nebo** A mountain east of the north end of the Dead Sea, in Moab. Before he died, Moses climbed Mt Nebo and saw the whole of the Promised Land spread out before him. Jebel Osha (3640ft/1120m high) has a viewpoint from which it is possible to see as far north as Mt Hermon, as well as the Dead Sea and the Negev. This is probably Mt Nebo.
Deuteronomy 32:48–52; 34:1–5/*6; C5*

**Negev** A dry scrubland and desert area in the far south of Israel. The Negev merges with the Sinai Desert on the way to Egypt. Abraham and Isaac camped in various places in the Negev. So too did the Israelites, before they settled in Canaan.
Genesis 20:1; 24:62; Numbers 13:17; 21:1; Isaiah 30:6/*4*

**Nile** The great river of Egypt on which the country's whole economy depended. The Nile flows from Lake Victoria in the heart of Africa, about 3,500 miles/5,632km to the Mediterranean Sea. The fertile valley of the Nile (never more than about 12 miles/19km wide in Upper Egypt) is flanked on either side by desert. Every year the river

flooded its banks in spring, leaving behind a layer of fertile mud. Crops would grow wherever the water reached. Too high a flood meant destruction; too low a flood, starvation. The river was also a useful means of transporting goods from one part of the country to another. About 12 miles/19km north of modern Cairo the Nile divides into a western and an eastern branch. Between them is the flat marshy land known as the Delta.

The Nile features in the dreams of Joseph's pharaoh. The pharaoh at the time of Moses' birth ordered his people to drown all Hebrew boy babies in the Nile. Moses himself was hidden in a basket in the reeds at the river's edge. The Nile also features in the sequence of plagues sent by God when the pharaoh refused to free the Israelites. It is often mentioned by the prophets.
Genesis 41:1–36; Exodus 1:22; 2:3–10; 7:17–25; 8:1–15, etc.; Isaiah 18:2, etc./3

**Nineveh** An important city in Assyria, notably in King Sennacherib's reign. The Bible says that Nineveh was founded by Nimrod the hunter. The site certainly has a very long history, going back to about 4500 BC. From about 2300 BC the city had a temple to the goddess Ishtar.

Nineveh grew in importance from about 1250 BC, as Assyria's power increased. Several Assyrian kings had palaces there. Sennacherib undertook a great deal of rebuilding and other work.

The ancient city of Pergamum was dominated by the great altar of Zeus. The modern town lies at the foot of the steep hill.

Reliefs carved on the walls of his new palace show his victories, including the siege of Lachish in Judah. At Nineveh, too, archaeologists discovered a clay prism (the Taylor Prism) which describes how King Hezekiah was 'shut up like a bird' in Jerusalem.

Ashurbanipal, the next king but one, added to Nineveh's greatness. Whole libraries of inscribed tablets, including the *Epic of Gilgamesh* (containing a flood story) and the creation epic (*Enuma elish*), have been discovered at his palace and in the temple of Nabu. Nineveh fell to the Babylonians in 612 BC.

In the Bible, Jonah was sent to save Nineveh; Nahum prophesied against it.
Genesis 10:11; 2 Kings 19:36; Jonah 1:2; 3; Nahum 1:1; Luke 11:30/3

**Nob** When David escaped from King Saul's attempts to kill him, he received help from the priest Ahimelech at Nob. But one of the king's men told Saul, and he had the priests at Nob killed. Isaiah foretold that the Assyrians would camp at Nob and advance on Jerusalem. It seems that Nob was a strong place close to the city, perhaps at Mt Scopus, north of the Mount of Olives. There was still a settlement at Nob when Nehemiah was rebuilding Jerusalem.
1 Samuel 21 – 22; Isaiah 10:32; Nehemiah 11:32; compare Matthew 12:4; Mark 2:26; Luke 6:4/6; B5

**Olives** See *Mount of Olives.*

**On** An ancient city in Egypt, famous for its worship of the sun-god Rē. Joseph married the daughter of the priest of On, and they had two sons, Ephraim and Manasseh. On is mentioned later in the prophets, once by its Greek name 'Heliopolis' (city of the sun).
Genesis 41:45, 50; 46:20; Ezekiel 30:17; compare Isaiah 19:18; Jeremiah 43:13/4

**Ophir** A country famous for its gold. It may have been in South Arabia, or East Africa (Somalia), or even India.
1 Kings 9:28, etc.

**Paddan-aram** The area around Harran in north Mesopotamia (not named in *Good News Bible*). Abraham sent his servant to Paddan-aram to choose a wife for Isaac from the branch of the family which had settled there. Jacob later fled from Esau to his uncle Laban, who was living at Paddan-aram.
Genesis 25:20; 28:2/4

**Pamphylia** A region on the southwest coast of modern Turkey. The town of Perga, visited by Paul, was in Pamphylia. Jews from this region were in Jerusalem and heard Peter and the apostles on the Day of Pentecost.
Acts 2:10; 13:13/13

**Paphos** A town in the south-west of Cyprus. Paul visited Paphos on his first missionary journey. Here he met the magician Elymas; and the governor of the island, Sergius Paulus, believed God's message.
Acts 13:4–13/15

**Paran** A desert area near Kadesh-barnea, where Hagar's son Ishmael grew up. The Israelites passed through it after the exodus. From here they sent spies into Canaan.
Genesis 21:20; Numbers 10:12; 12:16; 13:1–16, etc./5

**Patmos** An island off the west coast of modern Turkey. The place where John had the visions

written down in the Book of Revelation.
Revelation 1:9/*15*

**Penuel/Peniel** A place near the River Jabbok, east of the Jordan, where Jacob wrestled with the angel.
Genesis 32:22–32/*6; C4*

**Perga** A town just inland from Antalya (Attalia) on the south coast of modern Turkey. Paul visited Perga on arrival from Cyprus on the first missionary journey, and again when he returned to the coast.
Acts 13:13; 14:25/*15*

**Pergamum** The administrative capital of the Roman province of Asia (west Turkey). The first temple to be dedicated to Rome and the Emperor Augustus was built at Pergamum in 29 BC. Pergamum was also the centre of the pagan cults of Zeus, Athena, and Dionysus. There was a centre of healing connected with the temple of Asclepius (a fourth great pagan cult).
Pergamum was one of the seven churches to which the letters in the Book of Revelation are addressed. The phrase 'where Satan has his throne' may refer to emperor worship. (Picture page 279.)
Revelation 1:11; 2:12–16/*15*

**Persia** The country which conquered Media and overthrew Babylon to establish an empire which continued until the con-

quests of Alexander the Great. See *Persians* and Map in Part 1: *Environment of the Bible.*
Daniel was in Babylon when the city was taken by the army of the Medes and Persians. Cyrus, king of Persia, allowed the Jews and other exiles to return to their homelands. The Jewish girl, Esther, became queen to the Persian King Xerxes 1 (Ahasuerus).
Daniel 5:29–30; 6; 8:20; 10:1; Ezra 1:1–11; Esther 1, etc./*3*

**Pharpar** See *Abana.*

**Philadelphia** A town in the Roman province of Asia (modern Alashehir, in western Turkey). Philadelphia was one of the seven churches of Asia to which the

A great many travellers in New Testament times, including Paul, were glad of the fine roads built by the Romans. This is the Egnatian Way, just outside Philippi in northern Greece.

letters in the Book of Revelation are addressed.
Revelation 1:11; 3:7–13/*15*

**Philippi** A town 8 miles/12km inland from Neapolis on the coast of Macedonia (northern Greece). It was named after Philip of Macedon. Philippi was annexed by the Romans in 168 BC. It was the site of a famous battle between Antony and Octavian (Augustus) against Brutus and Cassius in 42 BC. Some years later, Octavian made Philippi a Roman colony, which gave its people the same rights and privileges as any town on Italian soil.

Paul visited Philippi on his second missionary journey, after seeing a vision of a Macedonian man appealing to him for help. The first Christian church in Europe was established at Philippi. Paul and Silas were illegally imprisoned here but later released with an apology when they made it known that they were Roman citizens. The letter to the Philippians was written to the church at Philippi.
Acts 16:6–40; 20:6; Philippians 1:1, etc.; 1 Thessalonians 2:2/*13*

**Philistia** The land of the Philistines, on the coast of Israel. See *Philistines* and Map in Part 1: *Environment of the Bible* and Part 10: *Atlas of the Bible.*

**Phoenicia** A small state on the coast of Syria, north of Israel. Its chief towns were Tyre, Sidon and Byblos. See *Phoenicians* and Map in Part 1: *Environment of the Bible.* /*3*

**Phoenix** Paul's voyage to Rome was delayed by the wrong winds, and the ship was still only at the south coast of Crete when the summer sailing season ended. At a conference at Fair Havens the majority wanted to sail on to Phoenix (modern Finika), the safest harbour on that coast, for the winter. Paul advised against this, but they sailed, and were caught in a violent storm and shipwrecked.
Acts 27:12/*15*

**Phrygia** A land in the centre of Asia Minor (modern Turkey). Most of it was in the Roman province of Asia, but Paul visited the smaller district which belonged to the province of Galatia. The main cities of this district were 'Pisidian' Antioch and Iconium. Three other Phrygian cities are mentioned by name in the New Testament: Laodicea, Colossae and Hierapolis.
Acts 16:6; 18:23; Colossians 1:1; 4:13; Revelation 3:14–22/*13*

**Pisgah** One of the peaks of Mt Nebo.

**Pisidia** A mountainous inland area off the south coast of modern Turkey. Paul passed through this remote and dangerous region on his first missionary journey, on his way from Perga to Antioch.
Acts 13:14; 14:24/*13*

**Pithom** One of Pharaoh's two store-cities, built by Israelite slave labour. It lay east of the Nile Delta in Egypt. See also *Raamses*.
Exodus 11:1/5

**Pontus** The ancient name of the Black Sea, and so of the land along its south coast. This became a Roman province, stretching along most of the northern coast of Asia Minor (Turkey). This was one of the lands to which Peter sent his first letter. The Christian message may have reached Pontus very early, as Jews from there were in Jerusalem on the Day of Pentecost.
Acts 2:9; 18:2; 1 Peter 1:1/13

**Ptolemais** The Greek name of an ancient city on the coast of northern Israel; Old Testament Acco. Paul sailed here from Tyre on his last visit to Jerusalem, and spent a day with the Christians here. The city is now again known by its early name Akko (Acre), but has lost much of its importance since the growth of modern Haifa near by.
Judges 1:31; Acts 21:7
*(Acco)/14; B2*

**Put** An African country, probably part of Libya (as in some modern Bible versions).
Genesis 10:6; Jeremiah 46:9; Ezekiel 27:10, etc.

**Puteoli** The port near Naples in Italy where Paul landed on his way to Rome as a prisoner. The town is now called Pozzuoli.
Acts 28:13/15

**Raamses/Rameses** Egyptian city near the coast on the east side of the Nile Delta. Pharaoh Ramesses II had a palace here. Earlier this was the Hyksos pharaohs' northern capital, Avaris. Exodus records that the Israelites built the cities of Pithom and Raamses as supply centres for the king. It was from Raamses that they set out on their escape from Egypt.
Exodus 1:11/5

**Rabbah** The capital city of the Ammonites (see *Ammon*), sometimes also called Rabbath-Ammon. The Israelites defeated Og, king of Bashan, whose 'iron bed' (or coffin) was preserved in Rabbah. This territory east of the Jordan was given to the tribe of Gad. But it was still occupied by the Ammonites until David's general Joab captured Rabbah. When David fled from his rebellious son Absalom he received help from Rabbah. After Solomon's death Ammon seems to have become independent again, and to have been once more a cruel enemy. The prophets denounce the wickedness of Rabbah and prophesy its destruction.

The city later took the Greek name Philadelphia, and became one of the ten cities of the Decapolis (see *Decapolis*). The name of the ancient people, the Ammonites, is preserved in the modern name, Amman. It is now the capital of Jordan.
Deuteronomy 3:11; Joshua 13:25; 2 Samuel 11:1; 12:26–31; 17:27; 1 Chronicles 20:1–3; Jeremiah 49:2; Ezekiel 21:20; 25:5; Amos 1:14/7

**Ramah** A Hebrew name meaning 'height', and used of several towns on hills. Two of these are important in the Old Testament story.

One was at er-Râm, 5 miles/8 km north of Jerusalem. Near here the prophetess Deborah lived. This Ramah was later close to the border between Judah and Israel. It was captured and fortified by Baasha, king of Israel, and recaptured by Asa of Judah. Isaiah pictures the Assyrians approaching Jerusalem by way of Ramah. Later, when Jerusalem actually fell to the Babylonians, Jeremiah was set free at Ramah. The place was resettled after the exile in Babylon. Rachel's tomb was said to have been near Ramah, and Jeremiah spoke of her weeping for her children. Matthew refers to this prophecy about Ramah in his account of what happened after Jesus' birth.
Judges 4:5; 19:13; 1 Kings 15:17, 22; 2 Chronicles 16:1, 6; Jeremiah 31:15; 40:1; Isaiah 10:29; Ezra 2:26; Nehemiah 11:33; Matthew 2:18/6; B5

The second Ramah was about 12 miles/19km further northwest. It was probably the birthplace and home of the prophet Samuel, and may have been the same as New Testament Arimathea. It was also called Ramathaim-Zophim.
1 Samuel 1:1; 2:11, etc./6; B4

**Ramoth-gilead** A city of refuge east of the Jordan which changed hands several times in the wars between Israel and Syria. It may be the same as Mizpah in Gilead, and so the home of Jephthah at the time of the Judges. One of Solomon's twelve district governors was stationed at Ramoth. King Ahab of Israel was killed in battle here. And Jehu was anointed king.
Joshua 20:8; Judges 11; 1 Kings 4:13; 22; 2 Kings 9:1–10/6; D3

**Red Sea** The meaning of the Hebrew word translated Red Sea is 'sea of reeds'. In the story of the exodus it refers to the area of lakes and marshes between the head of the Gulf of Suez and the Mediterranean Sea (the Suez

The forum, the city-centre of ancient Rome, at the heart of the Empire. Today we see only fragments of once-magnificent public buildings.

Canal area). It is also used for the Gulf of Suez, the Gulf of Aqaba (the northern arms of the Red Sea proper) as some modern Bible versions make plain.
Exodus 13, etc.; Numbers 33:10; Deuteronomy 1:40/3

**Rephaim** The valley where King David fought and defeated the Philistines. Also the name of one of the peoples who lived in Canaan before the Israelite conquest.
2 Samuel 5:18, etc.

**Reuben** Land belonging to the tribe of Reuben, east of the Dead Sea.
Joshua 13:15–23/5

**Rhegium** A port on the toe of Italy, on the Strait of Messina opposite Sicily; the modern city of Reggio di Calabria. Paul's ship called here on his voyage to Rome.
Acts 28:13/*15*

**Riblah** A town in Syria on the River Orontes. King Jehoahaz of Judah was taken prisoner at Riblah by Pharaoh Neco of Egypt. Later, King Nebuchadnezzar of Babylon had his headquarters here. And King Zedekiah, the last king of Judah, was taken to him at Riblah for sentence following rebellion.
2 Kings 23:33; 25:6–7/*10*

**Rome** Capital of the Roman Empire; on the River Tiber in Italy. The traditional date for the founding of Rome is 753 BC. The city spread over seven hills.

In New Testament times over a million people from all parts of the Empire lived in Rome, most of them in crowded multi-storey housing. The emperor and his government provided subsidies and public entertainments to keep the masses happy. The city attracted wealth, products – and writers and artists – from all over the Empire. Great Roman roads from every part of the Empire led here. There was a busy trade in foodstuffs and in luxury goods through the nearby port of Ostia. In Rome the emperors built some of the most magnificent public buildings any city has ever possessed.

There were Jews from Rome in Jerusalem on the Day of Pentecost who heard Peter's message. Although Paul did not visit Rome until the time of his imprisonment and appeal to Caesar, there seems to have been a Christian group there quite early. Aquila and Prisca, the Christian couple whom Paul met at Corinth, had come from Rome. They had probably been forced to leave when the Emperor Claudius expelled all the Jews from his capital. The letter to the Romans names a number of Christians in Rome already known to Paul. And there were friends to meet him after his voyage from Caesarea. He was in Rome under guard for two years

The harbour at Sidon, a flourishing centre of trade and commerce many centuries ago, in Phoenician times.

and during that time may have written a number of his letters to Christians in other places.

Tradition has it that Peter worked in Rome and, with Paul, was martyred here. There were certainly a great many Christians in Rome by AD 64, when the Emperor Nero began a cruel massacre. The evil and corruption of Rome are referred to in Revelation, where the city ('great Babylon') is pictured as a prostitute drunk with the blood of God's people. See *Romans* in Part 1: *Environment of the Bible.* (Picture page 281.)
Acts 2:10; 18:2; 19:21; 28:14–30; Romans 1:7, 15; 16; 2 Timothy 1:16–17; Revelation 17:5–18, etc./*13*

**Salamis** A commercial centre on the east coast of Cyprus. A number of Jews lived here, and when Paul visited the town he preached in synagogues.
Acts 13:5/*15*

**Salem** See *Jerusalem.*

**Salt Sea** The Old Testament name for the Dead Sea, given because the water contains very heavy deposits of salt. See *Arabah.*

**Samaria** Capital of the northern kingdom of Israel. The city was on the main north/south trade-route through Israel and was built on top of a hill so that it could easily be defended. The work of building the city was started about 875 BC by King Omri. It was continued by his son Ahab, who added a new palace. So much carved ivory was used to decorate the palace that it became known as the 'ivory house'. Over 500 pieces of ivory, some covered with gold leaf, have been discovered by archaeologists in the ruins of the palace.

From the start, the people of Samaria followed pagan religions. Several Old Testament prophets condemned their idol-worship and warned that the city would be destroyed.

The Syrians attacked and besieged Samaria many times, but it was the Assyrians who finally captured the city in 722/1 BC. The people were exiled to Syria,

Assyria and Babylonia. They were replaced by colonists from different parts of the Assyrian Empire. When Samaria fell, the kingdom of Israel ceased to exist. The whole area, not just the city, became known as Samaria.

By New Testament times the city of Samaria had been rebuilt by Herod the Great and renamed Sebaste (Greek for Augustus). A few half-caste Jews still remained in Samaria and claimed to worship God there, but these 'Samaritans' were despised and hated by the Jews in Judea. Jesus showed his concern for them by travelling through their land and staying with them. After Jesus' death and resurrection Philip went to Samaria to preach the gospel, and his work was followed up by Peter and John.

A small group of Samaritans still live in Nablus and Jaffa and worship on Mt Gerizim.
1 Kings 16:24, 32; Isaiah 8:4; Amos 3:8; 2 Kings 6:8 – 7:17; Luke 17:11; John 4:1–43; Acts 8:5–25/*6; B4*

**Sardis** A city in the Roman province of Asia (in modern Turkey) situated at the point where two main trade-routes met. In Roman times there were thriving dyeing and woollen industries here. One of the seven letters to churches in Asia, in the Book of Revelation, was addressed to the Christians at Sardis. The church had become apathetic. They relied on the past instead of concentrating on the present – an attitude typical of the city as a whole. It had been the capital of the kingdom of Lydia and at one time ruled by Croesus. His wealth was legendary; gold was easily obtained from a river which flowed close to the city. The first gold and silver coins were minted at Sardis.
Revelation 1:11; 3:1–6/*15*

**Seir** Another name for Edom.

**Sela** Capital of Edom. The name means 'rock' or 'cliff' and was given to this fortress-city because it was built on a rocky plateau high up in the mountains of Edom. About 300 BC the Nabataeans took Sela and carved the city of Petra (the Greek word for rock) out of the rocky valley at the foot of the original settlement.
2 Kings 14:7; Isaiah 16:1; 42:11/*13 (Petra)*

**Seleucia (Seleucia Pieria)** The port of Antioch in Syria. It was built by, and named after, the first Seleucid king. Paul and Barnabas

Glazed bricks with a winged bull inlaid; from the palace of Darius I at Susa, sixth century BC.

set sail from here for Cyprus on their first missionary journey.
Acts 13:4/*15*

**Senir** Another name for Mt Hermon. It is also used to describe a nearby peak and sometimes the whole range of mountains.

**Sepharvaim** A town as yet unidentified, captured by the Assyrians. People from here were brought to Samaria after the Jews had been sent into exile.
2 Kings 17:24, 31; 18:34

**Sharon** The coastal plain of Israel. It extends from Joppa to Caesarea – about 50 miles/80 km and is about 10 miles/16 km wide. Today the plain is one of the richest agricultural areas in Israel. In Bible times few people lived here. The land was used as pasture for sheep, but much of it was left in its natural state of thick scrub. The writer of the Song of Solomon (Songs) refers to the 'rose of Sharon', one of the many beautiful wild flowers which grew on the plain.
1 Chronicles 27:29; Song of Solomon (Songs) 2:1/*1*

**Sheba** A country in south-west Arabia, now the Yemen. Sheba became a wealthy land by trading spices, gold and jewels with the Mediterranean world. In the tenth century BC a queen of Sheba travelled over 1,000 miles/1,600

km by camel caravan to visit King Solomon and test his wisdom. She possibly also wished to arrange a trade agreement. The remains of a great dam and a temple to the moon-god Ilumquh have been discovered at Marib, once the capital of Sheba.
Psalm 72:15; Isaiah 60:6;
1 Kings 10:1–10, 13

**Shechem** An ancient Canaanite town which became an important religious and political centre for the Israelites; in the hill-country of Ephraim, near Mt Gerizim.

Abraham stopped at Shechem on his journey from Harran to Canaan. While he was here God told him, 'This is the country that I am going to give to your descendants.' Jacob also visited Shechem and set up camp outside the town.

When the Israelites had conquered Canaan Joshua gathered all the tribes together at Shechem. Here they renewed their promise to worship the God who had rescued them from Egypt, and to have nothing to do with foreign gods. But in the time of the Judges Canaanite worship was practised in Shechem. The inhabitants of the town gave Gideon's son Abimelech money from the temple of Baal-berith so that he could pay to have his seventy brothers killed. Abimelech made himself king of Shechem but the people soon turned against him. In revenge he destroyed the town.

After the death of King Solomon ten of the Israelite tribes rejected Solomon's son Rehoboam at Shechem. Jeroboam, the first king of the new northern kingdom, started to rebuild Shechem, and for a short time made it his capital.

Shechem survived the fall of Israel. It became the Samaritans' most important city and they built a temple here. A few Samaritans still live in Nablus, the modern town north-west of the site of Shechem.
Genesis 12:6–7; 33:18 – 35:4;
37:12–18; Joshua 24; Judges 9;
1 Kings 12/6; B4

**Shiloh** The town where the worship tent (tabernacle) was set up after the conquest of Canaan.

Shiloh became the centre of Israel's worship, and the tent was replaced by a more permanent building. Each year a special festival was held here. Hannah and Elkanah travelled to Shiloh to worship God. On one of these visits Hannah, praying for a son, promised that she would give him back to serve God. When Samuel was born Hannah kept her promise. She brought him back to Shiloh and he grew up in the temple, under the care of Eli the priest.

Archaeological evidence shows that Shiloh was destroyed about 1050 BC, probably by the Philistines. Jeremiah the prophet warned that the temple in Jerusalem would be destroyed just as the place of worship at Shiloh had been. But it seems that some people lived on the site of Shiloh, at least until the time of the exile.
Joshua 18:1; Judges 21:19;
1 Samuel 1 – 4; Jeremiah 7:12;
41:5/6; B4

**Shinar** Another name for Babylonia. See *Babylon.*

**Shittim** A place on the plains of Moab, across the Jordan from Jericho, also known as Abel-shittim, 'field of acacias'. The Israelites camped here just before they crossed the River Jordan into Canaan. They were probably at Shittim when the king of Moab tried to persuade Balaam to curse them. Preparations were made here for the conquest of Canaan. A census was taken of men able to fight; Joshua was chosen as Moses' successor; and two men were sent to spy out Jericho.
Numbers 25:1; 22 – 24; 26;

27:12–23; Joshua 2; 3:1;
Joel 3:18/6; C5

**Shunem** A place in the Valley of Jezreel, in northern Israel, modern Sôlem. The Philistines camped here before the battle on Mt Gilboa when Saul and Jonathan were killed. Elisha was the guest of a woman of Shunem, and he restored her child to life. The girl Abishag, who served David in his old age, was also a Shunnamite. The young woman called a 'Shulammite' in the Song of Solomon (Songs) may have come from the same place.
Joshua 19:18; 1 Samuel 28:4;
1 Kings 1 – 2; 2 Kings 4:8–37;
Song of Solomon (Songs) 6:13
/6; B3

**Shur** A desert area in the north-west part of the Sinai peninsula. Traders followed the 'Way of Shur' across the desert towards Egypt. Hagar fled this way after Sarah had treated her unkindly. When the Israelites had crossed the Sea of Reeds after escaping from Egypt they had to travel through this desert, and complained bitterly about the lack of water.
Genesis 16; Exodus 15:22–25/5

**Siddim** A valley (probably now submerged at the southern end of the Dead Sea) where Chedorlaomer, king of Elam, fought against the kings of the plain. During the fighting, Lot was taken prisoner, but he was rescued by Abraham.
Genesis 14

**Sidon** A Phoenician (Canaanite) port on the coast of modern Lebanon. Many skilled craftsmen worked in Sidon. Carved ivory, gold and silver jewellery and

Syria: a small village in the dry and dusty area north of Damascus.

beautiful glassware were among its exports. Each Phoenician city was virtually self-governing.

When the Israelites conquered Canaan they failed to take Sidon. In the time of the Judges the people of Sidon attacked and harassed the Israelites. The cultures began to merge and the Israelites were accused of worshipping the gods of Sidon – Baal and Ashtoreth. Jezebel, who promoted Baal worship in Israel, was the daughter of a king of Sidon. Because Sidon was opposed to Israel and the worship of God, the Old Testament prophets predicted the town's downfall. Sidon was captured, in turn, by Assyrians, the Babylonians and the Persians. Later it came under Greek and Roman control.

In the time of Jesus most of the inhabitants of Sidon were Greek. Many travelled to Galilee to hear him preach. Jesus also visited Sidon and the neighbouring city of Tyre. He compared Chorazin and Bethsaida, two towns in Galilee, with Tyre and Sidon, saying how much more readily the non-Jewish cities would have responded to him. Paul stopped at Sidon on his journey to Rome and stayed with friends in the city. (Picture page 282.)
Judges 1:31; 10:12, 6; 1 Kings 16:31; Isaiah 23:1–12; Ezekiel 28:20–24; Luke 6:17; Mark 7:24–31; Matthew 11:20–22; Acts 27:3, etc./7

**Siloam** A pool, originally underground, which was one of Jerusalem's main sources of water. The water in the pool came through a tunnel from the Gihon Spring outside Jerusalem. When the Assyrians threatened to besiege Jerusalem Hezekiah knew that in order to survive the city must have its own water supply, and gave orders for work on the tunnel. It is 1,750ft/538m long, cut through solid rock.

When Jesus healed a man who had been blind all his life he first put clay on his eyes and then told him to wash in the Pool of Siloam. The tower of Siloam which collapsed, killing eighteen people, probably stood on the slope of Mt Zion, above the pool.
2 Kings 20:20; John 9:1–12; Luke 13:4

**Simeon** The land given to the tribe of Simeon, in the Negev, the southernmost part of Israel. It seems that the area was considered an extension of Judah's territory.
Joshua 19:1–9; compare Joshua 15:20–32/5

**Sinai** A mountain in the Sinai peninsula and the area of desert around it. Three months after leaving Egypt the Israelites reached the mountain and set up camp. Here, at Mt Sinai, God gave Moses the Ten Commandments and other laws. The exact identification of Mt Sinai is not known. It was probably one of two peaks – Gebel Musa or Ras es-Safsafeh – in the south of the peninsula.
Exodus 19–32/5

**Smyrna** A port serving one of the main trade-routes across Asia. It is now the city of Izmir in modern Turkey. In New Testament times it was a beautiful city with many splendid public buildings. One of

them was the temple built in honour of the Emperor Tiberius, where emperor-worship was practised. One of the letters to the seven churches in the Book of Revelation is addressed to the Christians at Smyrna.
Revelation 1:11; 2:8–11/15

**Sodom** The town where Lot settled and which became notorious for its immorality. Sodom was suddenly destroyed, along with Gomorrah. Lot was warned of the impending disaster and escaped. Sodom probably now lies submerged at the southern end of the Dead Sea.
Genesis 13:8–13; 14; 19

**Succoth** 1. An Egyptian town. The Israelites made their first camp here on their journey out of the country.
Exodus 12:37; 13:20; Numbers 33:5–6/5

Ruins of the temple of Amon, at Karnak, Thebes, in Egypt.

2. A town in the Jordan Valley which became part of the territory of Gad. Jacob stayed for a while in Succoth after he and his brother Esau agreed to go their separate ways. In the time of the Judges the people of Succoth refused to provide Gideon and his army with food while he was fighting the Midianites. When Gideon was victorious he returned and punished the town officials.
Joshua 13:24, 27; Genesis 33:12–17; Judges 8:4–16/6; C4

**Susa** Capital of the Elamite Empire until King Ashurbanipal of Assyria destroyed the city in 645 BC and exiled its inhabitants to Samaria. Under the Medes and Persians it once again became an important city. Darius I built a splendid palace here. The ruins, in modern Iran, can still be seen. (Picture page 283.)

The story of Esther, the Jewish girl who became queen of Persia, took place at the royal court in Susa. It was here, too, that Nehemiah acted as royal cupbearer. The city was later captured by Alexander the Great.
Ezra 4:9–10; Esther 1:2, etc.; Nehemiah 1:1/3

**Sychar** A Samaritan town close to Jacob's well, where Jesus met and talked to a Samaritan woman who had come to draw water. Many people from Sychar believed Jesus was the Messiah when they heard what the woman said about him. The exact site is unknown.
John 4:1–42

**Syene** A place on the southern border of Egypt; modern Aswan. Isaiah pictures dispersed Jews returning to Jerusalem from as far away as Syene. Papyrus deeds found here record activities of Jewish settlers about 450 BC (the Elephantine Papyri).
Isaiah 49:12; Ezekiel 29:10; 30:6

**Syracuse** An ancient city in Sicily, where Paul spent three days on the last stage of his voyage to Rome after shipwreck on Malta.
Acts 28:12/15

**Syria** In the Old Testament, Syria is the land occupied by the Aramaeans to the north and north-east of Israel. The capital of

Syria was Damascus. See *Aramaeans* and Map in Part 1: *Environment of the Bible* and Part 10: *Atlas of the Bible*. (Picture page 284.)

**Taanach** A Canaanite city on the edge of the Valley of Jezreel. Barak fought Sisera near Taanach. It became one of the cities of the Levites.
Joshua 12:21; 21:25; Judges 5:19; 1 Kings 4:12/6; B3

**Tabor** An 1800ft/550m steep-sided mountain rising from the Plain of Jezreel. The place where Barak gathered his army at the time of the Judges.
Judges 4; Psalm 89:12; Hosea 5:1/6; B3

**Tahpanhes** An Egyptian town in the east part of the Nile Delta. The prophet Jeremiah was taken to Tahpanhes after the fall of Jerusalem and probably died there.
Jeremiah 43:5–10; Ezekiel 30:18/5

**Tarshish** The distant place for which Jonah set sail when he disobeyed God's command to go to Nineveh. A source of silver, tin, iron and lead. It may be Tartessus in Spain. (Some modern Bible versions translate it as Spain.)
Jonah 1:3; Isaiah 23:6; Jeremiah 10:9; Ezekiel 27:12

**Tarsus** A town on the Cilician plain 10 miles/16km inland from the south coast of modern Turkey. An important university city in New Testament times, housing 500,000 people. Tarsus was a meeting-place of East and West, of Greek and Oriental. Paul was born at Tarsus and proud of it. He returned there not long after

Thessalonica in northern Greece. Only the Roman arch remains to show that this busy modern street follows the route of the famous Roman Egnatian Way.

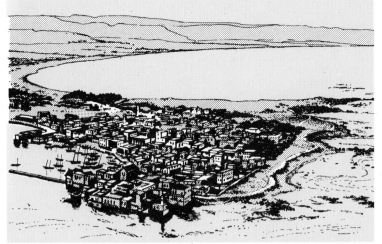

becoming a Christian. But Barnabas brought him to Antioch to help teach the new Christians.
Acts 9:11; 21:39; 22:3; 9:30; 11:25–26/*13*

**Tekoa** A town in the Judean hills about 6 miles/10km south of Bethlehem. A wise woman from Tekoa pleaded with King David to allow his son Absalom to come back to Jerusalem. Tekoa was also the home of the prophet Amos.
2 Samuel 14:2, etc.; Amos 1:1/*6; B5*

**Teman** Part of Edom. The people of Teman were famous for their wisdom. It was the home area of Job's friend Eliphaz.
Jeremiah 49:7; Job 2:11

**Thebes** The ancient capital city of upper Egypt, on the River Nile about 330 miles/531km south of modern Cairo. Two great temples of the god Amun (Karnak and Luxor) mark the site. From about 1500–1000 BC, when Amun was the official god of the Egyptian Empire, wealth and treasures poured into Thebes. But despite the city's remoteness it fell to the Assyrian King Ashurbanipal in 663 BC. The prophets Jeremiah and Ezekiel pronounced judgement on Thebes (No-Amon) and other Egyptian cities. (Picture page 285.)
Nahum 3:8–10; Jeremiah 46:25; Ezekiel 30:14–19/*3*

**Thessalonica** The chief city of Macedonia (northern Greece), on the Egnatian Way, the main Roman road to the East. Thessalonica (now Thessaloniki) is still a major city. Paul visited Thessalonica on his second missionary

A drawing of the island city of Tyre in Lebanon, seen from the air. The island part of the city has been linked to the mainland part since the engineers of Alexander the Great built the causeway which enabled him to capture the city.

journey. But the anger of the Jews forced him to move on to Beroea. His two letters to the Thessalonian Christians were written soon after he left.
Acts 17:1–15; 20:4; 27:2; Philippians 4:16; 1 Thessalonians 1:1; 2 Thessalonians 1:1, etc.; 2 Timothy 4:10/*13*

**Thyatira** A town in the Roman province of Asia (now Akhisar in west Turkey). Thyatira was a manufacturing centre for dyeing, clothes-making, pottery and brasswork. Lydia, the business woman from Thyatira who became a Christian when she met Paul at Philippi, was a 'dealer in purple cloth'. One of the seven letters in the Book of Revelation was addressed to the church at Thyatira.
Acts 16:14–15; Revelation 1:11; 2:18–29/*15*

**Tiberias** A spa town on the west shore of Lake Galilee. It was founded by King Herod Antipas and named after the Roman Emperor Tiberius. It was a non-Jewish town, and there is no record that Jesus ever went there. Tiberias is still a sizeable town today, unlike all the other lakeside places mentioned in the Gospels.
John 6:23/*14;C2*

**Tigris** The second great river of Mesopotamia. The Tigris rises in the mountains of eastern Turkey

and flows for more than 1,400 miles/2250km, joining the River Euphrates 40 miles/64km from its mouth on the Persian Gulf. The Tigris floods in spring and autumn. The great Assyrian cities of Nineveh, Calah and Assur were all built on the banks of the Tigris. The Bible mentions it as one of the four rivers of Eden.
Genesis 2:14; Daniel 10:4/*3*

**Timnah** A town on the northern boundary of Judah which fell into Philistine hands. The home of Samson's wife.
Judges 14/*6; A5*

**Timnath-serah, Timnath-heres** The town which Joshua received as his own. He was later buried here. The place was in the hill-country of Ephraim, north-west of Jerusalem.
Joshua 19:50; 24:30; Judges 2:9/*6; B4*

**Tirzah** A town in northern Israel, noted for its beauty. It was one of the places captured by Joshua. Later it was the home of Jeroboam I, and the first capital of the northern kingdom of Israel. King Omri later moved the centre of government to his new city of Samaria. The site of Tirzah is Tell el-Far'ah about 7 miles/11km north-east of Shechem (Nablus).
Joshua 12:24; 1 Kings 14–16; 2 Kings 15:14, 16; Song of Solomon (Songs) 6:4/*6; B4*

**Tishbe** The place from which Elijah, 'the Tishbite', presumably came. It was in Gilead, east of the Jordan, but the actual site is unknown.
1 Kings 17:1, etc.

**Tob** A region south of Damascus. At the time of the Judges Jephthah lived there as an outlaw. The people of Tob helped the Ammonites against David.
Judges 11:3; 2 Samuel 10:6/*7*

**Topheth** The place in the Valley of Hinnom where children were sacrificed. The shrine was destroyed by King Josiah.
2 Kings 23:10; Jeremiah 7:31; 19:6, 11–14

**Trachonitis** A district linked with Ituraea (see *Ituraea*). Together they made up the territory ruled

by Herod Philip at the time when John the Baptist began his preaching. Trachonitis was a rocky volcanic area, the haunt of outlaws, east of Galilee and south of Damascus.
Luke 3:1/*14; D2*

**Troas** A port about 10 miles/16km from Troy, in what is now north-west Turkey. Paul used the port a number of times on his travels. It was at Troas that

Drawing of a partial reconstruction of the great ziggurat (temple-tower) of Ur.

he had his vision of a Macedonian man calling for help, and he sailed from there on his first mission to Europe. On a later visit to Troas he restored Eutychus to life after he had fallen from an upstairs window while Paul was preaching.
Acts 16:8–12; 20:5–12;
2 Corinthians 2:12; 2 Timothy 4:13/*13*

**Tyre** An important port and city-state on the coast of Lebanon. Tyre had two harbours, one on the mainland, the other on an off-shore island. In about 1200 BC the Philistines plundered Sidon, the other important Phoenician port 20 miles/32km or so to the north. From that time on Tyre became the leading city.
  Tyre's 'golden age' was the time of David and Solomon. King Hiram of Tyre supplied wood and skilled men to build the temple at Jerusalem. Trade flourished. Tyre's own specialities were glass-ware and fine-quality purple dye made from local sea-snails.
  King Ahab of Israel married the daughter of the king of Tyre. The city is often mentioned in the Psalms and by the prophets, who condemned Tyre's pride and luxury. In the ninth century BC Tyre came under pressure from the Assyrians. The city paid heavy tribute in return for a measure of freedom. In the same year as the fall of Samaria, Sargon II of Assyria captured Tyre. When Assyria lost power Tyre became free and prosperous again. For thirteen years (587–574 BC), King Nebuchadnezzar of Babylon besieged the city. In 332 BC Alexander the Great managed to take the island port by building a causeway from the mainland.
  In New Testament times Jesus himself visited the area around Tyre and Sidon and spoke to the people. See also *Phoenicians* in Part 1: *Environment of the Bible.* (Picture page 287.)

2 Samuel 5:11; 1 Kings 5; 9:10–14; 16:31; Psalm 45:12; Isaiah 23; Ezekiel 26; Matthew 15:21; Luke 6:17; Acts 21:3 /*6; B1*

**Ur** A famous city on the River Euphrates in south Babylonia (modern Iraq); the home of Abraham's family before they moved north to Harran. The site of Ur had been occupied for several thousand years before it was finally abandoned about 300 BC. Excavations have uncovered thousands of inscribed clay tablets describing the city's history and life. The Royal Graves (about 2600 BC) contained many treasures, examples of beautiful craftsmanship: gold weapons, an inlaid mosaic gaming-board, the famous mosaic standard showing scenes of peace and war, and many other things. Ruins of a great stepped temple tower (ziggurat) still remain. See Part 2: *Archaeology and the Bible.*
Genesis 11:28–31, etc./*4*

**Uz** The home country of Job, probably in the region of Edom.
Job 1:1

**Zarephath/Sarepta** A small town that belonged to Sidon, later to Tyre. The prophet Elijah stayed with a widow there during a time of drought. Later he restored the widow's son to life.
1 Kings 17:8–24; Luke 4:26/*8*

**Zeboiim** One of a group of five early cities, of which the most famous are Sodom and Gomorrah. See *Admah, Sodom, Gomorrah.*
  Zeboiim was also the name of a valley near Michmash, in the desert north-east of Jerusalem, the site of a Philistine raid in the days of Saul.
Genesis 14:2, 8; Deuteronomy 29:23; 1 Samuel 13:18

**Zebulun** Land belonging to the tribe of Zebulun, in Galilee.
Joshua 19:10–16/*5*

**Ziklag** A town in the south of Judah taken by the Philistine city of Gath. King Achish of Gath gave it to David when he was an outlaw from King Saul. David recovered the captives after Amalekites had raided the town.
Joshua 15:31; 1 Samuel 27:6; 30 /*6; A6*

**Zin** An area of desert near Kadesh-barnea where the Israelites camped after the exodus.
Numbers 13:21; 20:1; 27:14, etc. /*5*

**Zion** The fortified hill which David captured from the Jebusites to make it his capital, Jerusalem. The name is often used in the Psalms and by the prophets.

**Ziph** A town belonging to the tribe of Judah, in the hills south-east of Hebron. David hid from Saul in the desert near Ziph, and Jonathan came to encourage him here. But the men of Ziph betrayed him to Saul, and he moved to Maon and Engedi. Later, Ziph was one of the places fortified by King Rehoboam. The site is still called Tell Zif.
Joshua 15:55; 1 Samuel 23:14–29; 2 Chronicles 11:9/*6; B6*

**Zoan/Tanis** An ancient Egyptian town in the north-east of the Nile Delta. From about 1100 to 660 BC Zoan was used as the capital of Egypt.
Numbers 13:22; Isaiah 19:11, etc./*5*

**Zoar** One of five cities probably at the southern end of the Dead Sea. Lot fled to Zoar at the time when Sodom was destroyed.
Genesis 13:10; 14:2, 8; 19:18–30

**Zobah** An Aramaean kingdom defeated by David; it was between Damascus and Hamath.
2 Samuel 8:3; 10:6; 1 Kings 11:23

**Zorah** Samson's birthplace.
Judges 13:2; 16:31/*6; A5*